Central Vermont Railroad

By-Ways

Central Vermont Railroad

By-Ways

ISBN/EAN: 9783743304369

Manufactured in Europe, USA, Canada, Australia, Japa

Cover: Foto ©Thomas Meinert / pixelio.de

Manufactured and distributed by brebook publishing software
(www.brebook.com)

Central Vermont Railroad

By-Ways

CENTRAL VERMONT RAILROAD

-WAYS

BY-WAYS.

❖

ILLUSTRATED.

Aide Memoire of Popular Resorts Included in Tours.

Bellows Falls

from the riuer.

"OF the Green Mountains one might probably say, they are more generally admired than visited. Poets sing without seeing them. They have furnished ready and familiar figures to orators who could hardly point them out on the map. That they stimulate the virtues of the patriot is one of those axioms which one meets over and over again in the pages of writers who have never felt their rugged breezes. Nor is this service which the State furnishes to rhetoric shared in anything like an equal degree by other States which also have mountains loftier, perhaps, and grander than its own. Even the White Mountains seem to be less frequently used, while the Alleghanies, the Rocky Mountains, and other noble chains throughout the country, are almost unknown in literature and oratory. Only one thing, therefore, is wanting to complete the singular pre-eminence of Vermont. If her mountains and valleys were more often traversed and better known, the phrases of enthusiasm and admiration would not, perhaps, be subdued, but they would be

well-informed, just, rational, more serviceable to their authors, and not less complimentary to their objects."—*Harper's Magazine*, Nov., 1883.

"By-Ways" can, of course, repair this neglect only in part. To describe the whole State, or even all its leading beauties, would require a dozen volumes instead of as many pages. We shall, therefore, take for description some points in Vermont landscape reached by the Central Vermont Railroad, and then invite the reader with their aid to complete the picture.

A SUMMER EXCURSION

AMONG GREEN MOUNTAIN BY-WAYS.

"I have gathered a posy of other men's flowers, and nothing but the thread that binds them is mine own."

THERE is a best way to travel as there is a best way to live; and to know how to do either, one must have experience, or hints from the experienced. If you are hesitating as to which route you will take for a summer's jaunt or for a fishing excursion, or if you desire to pass the "heated term" among quiet mountain resorts,

and are in doubt which way to go, let me give you a hint; let me tell you about a few of the towns and cities you will pass through; let me give you a mere suggestion of the beautiful scenery which meets the eye on every hand, and a word about the comforts of a journey through the Green Mountains.

A bright day in the middle of May and a little leisure, suggested a short railway trip, and a friend whispered in my ear, "Take your outing over the Central Vermont Railroad, and you will not regret your choice; as you will not suffer from excessive heat nor a dusty road, and finer bits of scenery cannot be seen from any road in the country, than are visible along this route."

Before I returned home I echoed my friend's sentiments concerning the scenery; for it must be a dullard, indeed, who could not enjoy such a trip. A ride over this magnificent road, perfectly ballasted, supplied with the best steel rails, its bridges of stone or iron, and the cars fitted with every imaginable appliance to promote the comfort and safety of the public, is a desideratum, and not an experience to be dreaded.

Leaving Boston at 8.30 a.m. or 1.00 p.m., we glide (I use that word, for the motion is scarcely perceptible) past the few suburban towns intervening between Boston and Winchester, and halt here for a few moments. Our next halting place is

Lowell, where baggage is taken on and put off, and we have time to make a few inquiries concerning the "city of spindles" and the home of General Butler. In 1880, Lowell had a population of 59,475—a gain over the previous ten years of 18,547. It is the leading cotton-manufacturing city in the United States, and is also a railway junction, six roads centring here. The territory of the city embraces 2,587 acres. The first cotton-mill was erected here in 1820. To-day there are eighty mills, in which is invested over twenty millions of capital.

Along the Merrimack.—Leaving Lowell, we ride for forty or fifty miles along the bank of the Merrimack, which, rising in the town of Franklin. N. H., from the Pemigewasset and the Winnipiseogee, flows peacefully on until lost in the Atlantic. The ride along the river is particularly enjoyable. Here one could toss a stone into the water, then by a sudden turn in the stream or road we lose sight of it for a minute, and soon we catch the glow of its ripples, sparkling in the sunlight across the mile of fertile meadow-land, the high, yellow, sandy banks furnishing a frame of old gold for the dark, sparkling river, which flows peacefully on to its destination, save where here and there protruding rocks disturb the even tenor of its way. But our meditations are cut short by a brief halt at

Nashua, which is the junction of several railways. This little city is not, like Lowell, Lawrence and Manchester, distinguished as a manufacturing centre, although it boasts of a number of very successful business enterprises. It is a pretty place, has an area of 18,898 acres, and in 1880 had a population of 15,397. The Merrimack enters the city from the east, and the Nashua River from the west; it has also the Salmon Brook on the south, and the North Penni-chuck Brook on the north, and all these streams are utilized for manufacturing purposes.

Manchester is our next stopping place, and as the train runs into the commodious station, one is impressed with the activity and bustle of the city, which in 1880 boasted a population of 32,630. From the windows of the car, as we hurry along toward the north, we catch glimpses of the large manufactories—the Amoskeag, the Stark, the Manchester, and the Langdon mills. There are also several minor manufactories here, and the noted Manchester Locomotive Works. Millions of dollars are invested in these establishments, which give employment to thousands of men, women and children. The city has a system of water-works which cost $800,000.

Concord.—Eighteen miles north of Manchester lies the capital city of the old Granite State, which in 1880 had a population of 13,838. It is one of the most interesting inland cities of New England. Its topography presents a wonderful variety, consisting of hills and wide-spreading intervales, winding rivers, swift rapids, and calmly nestling lakes. Through the centre of the city, from the north, flows the tortuous Merrimack, and the Contoocook enters from the north-west corner. The hills of Concord would in many States be desig-nated as mountains, for one—the "Rattlesnake"—rises from near the centre of the city to a height of 500 feet above the river. The city contains the State House, State Prison, Insane Asylum, the County Jail, White's Opera House, eleven churches, three newspapers, four hotels, seven banks, and several manufacturing establishments, although the city is better known for wealth and politics than on account of its manufactures.

From Concord to White River Junction the ride is full of interest, aside from the pleasures of the landscape. Seven miles from Concord we pass the village of Fisherville, and are reminded of

Hannah Duston, a brave woman, whose courage and endurance are told to the world in a monument which was erected to her memory, a few years ago, by the New Hampshire Historical Society. Hannah Duston lived in Haverhill, Mass. She was the mother of thirteen children, the youngest a babe of a few months, when on the 15th day of May, 1698, the Indians descended on the settlement, and after slaughtering many of the inhabitants, carried Hannah, her child and nurse, off as prisoners. The child was killed, and the two women were taken to an island in the Merrimack, near the mouth of the Contoocook, now known as Duston's Island. She was held a prisoner there in a company of twelve savages. One night, with the aid of her nurse and a white boy, this brave and determined woman killed all the Indians in their sleep, except one squaw, took their scalps, and after a journey fraught with peril, hunger, and hardship, the trio found their way back to Haverhill.

The Home of Webster.—The place where the great "expounder" passed so many happy hours in his youth and manhood was pointed out to us as we hurried through Webster Place, a small village. The large white house not far from the railroad track was where he lived for a good many years, and his birthplace is not far distant, in the town of Salisbury, which, when Webster was born, was a part of the town of Franklin, and both towns claim the honor of giving to the world the great statesman. We halt for a few moments at Franklin, a pretty place, situated on both sides of the Merrimack; and here we bid adieu to the stream which we have traced from Lowell, sixty-six miles. A little way beyond Franklin we skirt the shore of the pretty lake named after Webster, where he was accustomed to enjoy his favorite pastime—fishing. At Franklin the Bristol Branch Railway diverges from the main line, and runs to Bristol, thirteen miles.

Potter Place, a station about two miles north of Franklin, is our next halting-place, and here we remain long enough to get a good view of Mount Kearsage, a noted summer resort.

The Enfield Shakers.—We rush along, passing Canaan, Enfield, Lebanon, and West Lebanon. Enfield calls for rather more than a passing glance, for it is situated in the midst of scenery of surpassing loveliness, and is the home of a peculiar people. The Enfield Shakers have a wide reputation. Shaker flannels, garden-seeds, apple-sauce, pails, brooms, etc., are familiar to nearly every New England boy and girl. Just north of this prosy, industrious village, where poetry seems to have been forgotten by this matter-of-fact people, we suddenly come upon the loveliest little lake imaginable, and skirt its shores for miles. Framed in a cluster of sheltering hills, it ripples and dances to the music of the breeze, and, as it glistens and smiles beneath the sun, it sorely tempts the lover of nature to quit the busy, bustling, selfish world, and, like Thoreau upon the shores of Walden, commune with the Unseen, and dream his life away. But steam and time will not pause for us to grow sentimental, and we rush along past Lebanon and West Lebanon toward the Junction. The large building on the hill overlooking West Lebanon, is the Tilden Seminary for young ladies. We cross the Connecticut over an immensely high bridge, and are at

White River Junction.—"Twenty minutes for refresh-

145 MILES FROM BOSTON.
140 MILES FROM NEW YORK.
170 MILES FROM MONTREAL.

ments!" is welcomed by the hungry passengers, some of whom leave us here, and after lunch at the restaurant, take trains for Springfield, Bellows Falls, and other points along the connecting lines of road.

We have been riding thus far since leaving Boston over the Boston and Lowell (Southern Division), the Concord, and the Northern Division Boston and Lowell Railroad. At White River Junction we begin our ride over the Central Vermont proper. This road was opened to Montpelier in 1849, and to Burlington in 1850. In 1852 the route was extended to Montreal, via Rouse's Point, and in 1862 the present route to St. Johns and Montreal was opened.

After leaving White River Junction we ride along the bank of the White River, the clearness and purity of whose waters are quite remarkable. It is said the stream derived its name from the great number of white pebbles on its bed. This led the Indians to call it "Kascadnac," which has been Anglicized as White River.

The scenery along this route from White River Junction to St.
Albans is of the most delightful character. The White River and
Winooski Valleys present to the eye of the tourist pictures of the
rarest loveliness. The deep, fertile valleys, the gently sloping uplands, the verdant hillsides, the cloud-capped summits of the grand
old rock-bound hills, combine to furnish scenery unsurpassed in this
country in peaceful beauty and grandeur. I know of no railway
route where more beautiful, impressive and charming scenery can be
found than over the Central Vermont and its numerous branches.
Fresh surprises greet the traveler on every hand, until, at the end
of a day's journey, one retraces his way over the mountains, through

the valleys, over the rushing torrents, past the peaceful, prosperous farms, where contentment reigns supreme, along the fertile meadows, beside the loveliest of lakes, through prosperous villages and rocky gorges, and the mind is lost in wonder that the skill of man should have placed it in one's power to witness such magnificent panoramas with ease and comfort. Immediately after leaving the junction we pass

Hartford, situated in the midst of a fine farming district, and possessed of valuable water-power. The township of Hartford has a population of about 2500. Ten miles southwest, and reached by the Woodstock R. R., is Woodstock, the shire town of Windsor County, beautifully located in the valley of the Otta Queechee.

147 MILES FROM BOSTON.
141 MILES FROM NEW YORK.
144 MILES FROM MONTREAL.

HARTLAND BRIDGE.

West Hartford is a small manufacturing village. The track

shortly crosses a brook, which breaks into a charming fall, to be seen on the right; and soon after we cross White River. From the bridge a beautiful view may be obtained. A valley opens to the

southward surrounded by picturesque sharp-crested hills, dotted with farms, and through the midst flow the transparent waters of the river, now breaking into foam over gray limestone ledges and now running swiftly over its smooth, pebbly bed. A short distance beyond is

Sharon, the birthplace of Joseph Smith, the founder of the

Mormon sect. The town was plundered by Indians in 1780, on the same day with the Royalton massacre. Many brooks "join the brimming river" in this section, and the valleys through which they

Shovel Valley.

run may be seen winding among the green hills on either side of the railway. The train rushes past only too quickly, and soon brings us to

South Royalton, a neat and attractive village, standing on the side of a beautiful valley. Crossing the river on a bridge 600 feet long, we again follow its right bank to

171 MILES FROM BOSTON.
270 MILES FROM NEW YORK.
171 MILES FROM MONTREAL.

Royalton, pleasantly situated on the river bank, surrounded by fertile fields, and whose inhabitants were massacred by Indians in 1780 simultaneously with those of Sharon. Another short run brings us to

164 MILES FROM BOSTON.
263 MILES FROM NEW YORK.
169 MILES FROM MONTREAL.

Bethel, which is in a narrow valley, encircled by high and steep hills, and is the stage point for Barnard, Rochester and Hancock. These inland villages are situated at elevations ranging from 1000 to 1300 feet above the level of the sea, in the midst of picturesque valleys watered by numerous trout streams.

171 MILES FROM BOSTON.
264 MILES FROM NEW YORK.
161 MILES FROM MONTREAL.

Randolph.—The stranger is surprised on nearing this village at the evidence of prosperity and industry everywhere visible. The business part of the village was totally destroyed by fire in the autumn of 1884, but is being rapidly rebuilt. The surface of the country in the vicinity is elevated, but less broken than much of the surrounding territory. Soon after leaving the station we come in sight of the higher summits of the Green Mountains. The hillsides become more rugged, and rocks, showing a vertical stratification, lift their frowning precipices over the green fields at their base.

177 MILES FROM BOSTON.
707 MILES FROM NEW YORK.
184 MILES FROM MONTREAL.

Braintree is composed of a few houses, with a row of brick charcoal pits, shut in by rugged mountains, a few meadows along the river forming a foreground. A little further on at

183 MILES FROM BOSTON.
200 MILES FROM NEW YORK.
182 MILES FROM MONTREAL.

Roxbury, we cross the summit pass of the Green Mountains, at an elevation of one thousand feet above the sea, and leaving the headwaters of the White River, whose company we have enjoyed for about fifty miles, we strike the source of the Dog River, a tributary

188 MILES FROM BOSTON.
209 MILES FROM NEW YORK.
148 MILES FROM MONTREAL.

State Capitol

Depot of Central Vt R.R.

Central part of Montpelier Vt

of Lake Champlain. Just west of the station we cross a bridge seventy feet above the stream, which flows beneath, and begin our descent towards Lake Champlain. Seven miles from Roxbury we come upon

Northfield, where formerly were located the shops of the Central Vermont, which several years ago were removed to St. Albans. Two ranges of bold hills, one on each side of Dog River, render the surface of Northfield very uneven. The large brick building, with a Mansard roof, on the hill to the right, south of the station, is Lewis College, formerly the Vermont Military Institute. Ten miles beyond Northfield we arrive at

(margin: 170 MILES FROM BOSTON. 614 MILES FROM NEW YORK. 103 MILES FROM MONTREAL.)

Montpelier, or rather, we should say, Montpelier Junction, for a short spur track runs down from the village. Montpelier is one of the most beautiful towns in New England. It is nestled beneath high, verdant hills, which stand guard over a refined, cultured, and wealthy community—a community where law and order, peace and prosperity, education and refinement, have ever held sway. The population of the town is about four thousand. It is, as everybody knows, the capital of the State, and until the erection of the new State House at Albany, N. Y., only one other State, Ohio, boasted of so fine a State House as did Vermont. The edifice is built of granite, cruciform in its general plan; 176 feet long, and surmounted by a dome 124 feet high. In the portico, surrounded by Doric columns, stands a marble statue of Ethan Allen, of whose fame Vermont is justly proud. The Pavilion Hotel over-looking Capitol Park, upon which are the State Buildings, commands the most beautiful portion of the town, and is one of the best hotels in New England, being equipped with all the appurtenances essential to a first-class hotel. Extensive piazzas around the house afford delightful promenades and lounging places for summer guests. Few towns in New England can offer so many attractions to the denizen of the city who wishes to secure a quiet, restful, beautiful spot in which to pass his vacation. Its drives are delightful, its scenery entrancing, its people hospitable. It is one of the few places in the

(margin: 200 MILES FROM BOSTON. 575 MILES FROM NEW YORK. 113 MILES FROM MONTREAL.)

country where one can escape from the horrible "hay fever" with which so many are annually afflicted.

The Winooski Valley, into which the traveler is ushered as he enters Montpelier, is remarkable for its fertility and beauty. The broad, rich meadows, the gradually rising uplands, the verdant

SLIP HILL—MIDDLESEX.

hills, the craggy mountain peaks, form a picture rare, as the sun is seeking his rest and casting his shadows aslant the lovely landscape.

"Each purple peak, each flinty spire,
Is bathed in floods of living fire."

Middlesex.— Before reaching Middlesex, the river, now on the left, falls over a series of rocky ledges, then plunges into Middlesex Narrows, a cañon about a quarter of a mile in length and thirty feet in

215 MILES FROM BOSTON.
340 MILES FROM NEW YORK.
112 MILES FROM MONTREAL.

depth, which has been worn in the slaty rock by the action of the river. Eight miles from Montpelier we halt at

Camel's Hump
from South of
Waterbury Vt.

Waterbury, pleasantly situated on a pretty plateau. Camel's Hump looks over the intervening ridges as we near the station, and assumes an almost human expression, having the outline of a forehead

617 MILES FROM BOSTON.
296 MILES FROM NEW YORK.
112 MILES FROM MONTREAL.

and nose. The Waterbury Hotel is near the station, and has ample accommodation for a large number of guests. Waterbury is so attractive in its situation and surroundings that many summer tourists make it their headquarters. Mount Mansfield and Camel's Hump, the highest of the Green Mountain peaks, are within easy riding distance, and the whole vicinity is rich with the characteristic scenery of Vermont.

Mount Mansfield, five thousand feet high, is the principal attraction of this region, and is most conveniently reached from Stowe, ten miles north of Waterbury.

"The two hours' drive, especially if one has an outside seat, is no unpleasant experience on a July evening. It is the very heart of the Green Mountains. The road is good; the hills are neither too prolonged nor too abrupt. Enticing trout streams shoot across the way, or ripple along its side. Mount Mansfield and Camel's Hump are seen, now on one hand, now on the other, as we pursue our sinuous course. The farms are neat, orderly, and apparently prosperous.

"**Stowe** is a typical Vermont village, of some one thousand inhabitants. The houses are nearly all white, and the white houses nearly all have green shutters, though slight differences in the style of architecture and a modest discrimination in the choice of

flowers and the arrangement of flower-beds afford a partial satisfaction to the eye. There is a small white church, and its spire, or 'steeple,' as the parishioners call it, shoots ambitiously up into the clear blue air. The Mount Mansfield Hotel has lately been purchased by a stock company, and will be under an entirely new management. It has been thoroughly renovated, refurnished, and the grounds beautified. The hotel has rooms for 450 guests. They are large, high and cheerful, and are furnished in suites and private parlors. A broad veranda runs nearly the entire length of the front, 300 feet. From "Sunset Hill," a sharp elevation back of the hotel, the village resembles a flock of geese on the wing, the two main streets diverging toward the east and the west, while the apex, where the leader may be imagined, points timidly toward Waterbury on the south. Many other things may also be seen from Sunset Hill. In the rear is the Worcester range; south, Camel's Hump; west, Mount Mansfield itself; and in the intervals, especially toward the northwest, the green valley with its silver streams, its well stocked farms, its neat farm-houses, with their barns and other buildings grouped in little colonies about them. This is, too, a good point from which to begin the work of seeing a man's face in the profile of Mount Mansfield. The features are all there in bold relief—forehead, nose, mouth, lips, chin.

"The distance from Stowe to the summit is about nine miles. For five miles the route follows the ordinary country road through a pleasant valley; then it breaks off into the mountain, and winds about by easy grades to the top. The carriage road has now been open several years, and the ascent can be made in any vehicle with the greatest comfort. The way is thickly wooded—along the lower part with beach, maple, birch and even oak, which, however, gradually disappear until the evergreen varieties alone remain, and these seem ill satisfied with their existence. Shade is therefore abundant and the sun's rays are little felt. Half a mile before the summit is reached the woods open, and the carriage climbs a stiff rocky ledge for the rest of the way. The Nose towers up directly above us, and the other features stretch away in the distance, massive, solemn, and forbidding. The highest point, the Chin, is 4,359 feet above sea-level, and 3,670 above the village of Stowe.

"From the Chin the spectator has one of the most comprehensive, variegated and beautiful views to be found in all New England.

"Mt. Mansfield" from Sunset Hill.

Toward the west, the eye, starting from the base of the mountain, runs over the Winooski Valley, threaded by roads and streams, and dotted with countless white villages, the effect of which is both remarkable and pleasing; takes in Lake Champlain, which on a clear day can be seen for nearly its entire length; and is arrested only by the Adirondacks in the remote horizon. On the north the outlook is even more extensive, and at rare intervals, under peculiarly favorable atmospheric conditions, even includes the spires and

Summit House.

towers of Montreal, one hundred miles distant. Directly beneath and between the first and second chains, lies the Lake of the Clouds; lower down the dark recesses of the Smuggler's Notch, and across this the Sterling Mountains. Moving to the east, the eye falls upon a succession of dark and heavy ridges, thickly wooded, giving and receiving shadows in endless variety ; farther away, the valley of the Connecticut ; and beyond, the White Mountains, Mount Washington itself being sometimes seen, though indistinctly. The picture is completed by Stowe and its neighbors, nestling in the rich valley, and directly south the rival peak of Camel's Hump and the main chain of the Green Mountains. Such is, in general, the scope of the view afforded from Mount Mansfield. The countless details which give it grace, picturesqueness and value cannot even be enumerated, but must be left with the assurance that not one which the imagination could crave will be found wanting by the most exacting lover of nature.

"For loftiness, grandeur and majesty, Mount Mansfield is, of course, inferior to Mount Washington. Its charms are of a more modest nature. But it has, nevertheless, peculiar advantages of its own, which will not escape the eye of discerning visitors, and which will recommend it even above the White Mountains. One of these is the singular extent and freedom of the view which may be had from its summit. Instead of being only one of a vast army of peaks, distinguished from its comrades merely by a slight superiority in height, it is more like an isolated structure rising out of a surrounding plain. In at least two directions, east and west, the landscape is unobstructed for a hundred miles. The country lies spread out, therefore, in a vast plateau, beginning at the very base of the mountain, and enlivened by every element which belongs to a complete picture. The landscape itself is, therefore, an ample reward for the toil and expense of the visit.

"The neighborhood of Stowe affords a multitude of other charming resorts, some of which must at least be mentioned. One of these is the Smuggler's Notch, a narrow pass between Mount Mansfield and the Sterling Mountain. It is supposed to have been used in former times by smugglers, as it is an easy and convenient connection between eastern and western Vermont, and a link in the chain of communication between Montreal and Boston, once an important thoroughfare for contraband traffic. A good road, following the course of a noble trout stream, ends only at the Notch House, a deserted inn at the summit of the pass, and the source of

Moss Glen
Cascade

Williamstown Gulf
and Gulf Springs House

the stream, the Mammoth Spring, which is not improperly named.
Beyond the house a footpath leads through a succession of mighty
boulders which have fallen from the cliffs above, under abrupt
precipices which stretch up on either side to appalling heights, and

through damp ravines where the ferns grow in fantastic luxuriance and beauty."—*Harper's Magazine*, Nov., 1883.

> "With boughs that quaked at every breath
> Gray birch and aspen wept beneath:
> Aloft, the ash and warrior oak
> Cast anchor in the rifted rock;
> And higher yet the pine tree hung
> His shattered trunk, and frequent flung,
> Where seemed the cliffs to meet on high,
> His boughs athwart the narrowed sky;
> Highest of all where white peaks glanced,
> Where glistening streamers waved and danced,
> The wanderer's eye could barely view
> The summer heaven's delicious blue;
> So wondrous wild, the whole might seem
> The scenery of a fairy dream"

Other attractions are Moss Glen Cascade, only four miles from Stowe; Gold Brook, a favorite drive; Morrisville Falls and Johnson Falls, somewhat more distant, and various other choice rural nooks which will well repay a visit. The roads are, for mountain roads, uniformly good, and ladies unaccompanied ride in confidence and safety all over the country.

After our interesting ramble among these By-Ways we take the train at Waterbury, and a five-mile run brings us to

North Duxbury, located in a region thinly inhabited. Just before reaching the station a wild and rocky scene, known as Bolton Falls, opens to the northward. The wagon road from Waterbury to Bolton passes near by, and furnishes a favorite drive for those who are fortunate enough to spend any time in the vicinity. Beyond North Duxbury a constant succession of river pictures may be seen on the south side of the track, while ranges of wild and picturesque rocks rear themselves on the northern side. As the railway approaches

Richmond the country becomes more open, and is evidently richer in agricultural products than the more narrow, though fertile, valleys. Next to St. Albans, it sends to the Boston market the largest quantity of butter and cheese of any town in the State. The town lies just where the Winooski Valley opens into that of Lake Champlain, and combines in a most attractive manner the beauties of mountain and meadow. As the railway leaves the mountains the

view becomes more extended, and from the northern or right hand side of the car the noble outlines of rounded summits can be seen, while on the opposite side the distant Adirondacks soon come in sight, beyond Lake Champlain.

Williston is a farming town. Beyond the station we again cross the Winooski, and from the bridge obtain a full view of Mount

214 MILES FROM BOSTON.
313 MILES FROM NEW YORK.
99 MILES FROM MONTREAL.

Mansfield and Camel's Hump. These two mountains are in sight, at intervals, for many miles on this portion of the railroad, and the rather ill-proportioned human profile of the former may be seen to the best advantage.

Essex Junction has grown up since the railway

241 MILES FROM BOSTON.
300 MILES FROM NEW YORK.
94 MILES FROM MONTREAL.

connection with Burlington was made, a branch extending eight miles to that city, of which more anon. Leaving Essex Junction, we run through

MT. MANSFIELD FROM ESSEX.

Milton, a prosperous village situated on the Lamoille River.
The Great Falls of the Lamoille are within an
easy walk from the railway, and are worthy
a visit, though somewhat disfigured by the
"improvements" made for the purpose of controlling the water-
power. At

Georgia, the railway crosses the Lamoille on a bridge which
spans the river at a giddy height. Stage connection is made here for Fairfax, five miles
distant. A few minutes later the car door

opeps, and we are notified that we have reached

St. Albans, where fifteen minutes will be allowed for refreshments. St. Albans is a characteristic Yankee town, having a more cosmopolitan air, however, than most New England villages, due largely to the fact that the large construction and repair shops are located here. The lower part of the town, in the vicinity of the railway station, is level; but the land soon rises, and the principal business street, with the pleasantest part of the town, is built upon a gently sloping hill overlooking Lake Champlain, which will well repay a visit, being only two and a half miles distant. A couple of blocks from the depot the eye is pleasantly greeted by the spacious and rarely beautiful park which is, very appropriately, the focal part of the town. It is spangled with pathways leading beneath lofty and overspreading elms almost as dense and shady as those of the storied aisles of classic New Haven. A beautiful fountain, the gift of ex-Gov. J. Gregory Smith, has lately been placed in the park, costing $7,000, and being the finest in New England. One entire side of the park is faced by three churches, the court house and high school, and above the verdure which seems to fill the village, other spires peep out, proclaiming the healthy morality of the town; the balance of the quadrangle is filled with stores, shops, markets, and one or two hotels sufficiently commodious and well furnished to meet the requirements of the most fastidious.

The healthful climate, the pure air, and the delightful drives render St. Albans an unusually attractive summer resort; and it is safe to say that the admirer of rural loveliness cannot fail of being gratified with the profusion of Nature's beauties everywhere observable in this locality. The private residences (many of them environed with handsome, well-cared for foregrounds) constitute another charm.

All who have visited the place have heard of the magnificent view from Aldis Hill, an elevation near the town. It commands the ranges of the Adirondacks and Green Mountains, and a wide stretch of Lake Champlain. At the hour of sunset, on a calm evening, the beauty of the scene from this hill is entrancing.

Then there is the ride to Bellevue, a winding hillside road, rewarding the gazer, at the top of a neighboring eminence, with one

St. Albans from the Mountain.

of the most expansive views in the State, one which, as an artist would put it, "composes" well. Not far away the turrets of costly homes stand looking down upon the town, which spreads right and left, with a trio of spires marking the centre. Four miles away Champlain rests placidly, and is lost in the vague northern distance. Far beyond, the gray peaks of the Adirondacks dimly stain the western horizon. What mellow tones and effective neutral tints were revealed the May morning we looked upon this scene!

The drive to St. Albans Bay, an arm of the lake, is a matter of but two and a half miles, but may be extended along the bay to Hathaway's Point or the Lake View House. Abundant facilities for fishing may be found here, and piscatorial sport at this point, especially angling for bass and pike, is a matter of fame among those who love the rod and reel, the locality being known to them as the Great Back Bay.

Taking the train of the Missisquoi Railroad, a run of nine miles from St. Albans brings us to Congress Hall, Sheldon Springs, whose waters have effected so many noted cures of obstinate and chronic diseases. In front of

Congress Hall flows the Missisquoi River—the largest river in Vermont—and at this point is found a succession of falls, in all 119 feet. When at full banks it is an imposing stream, and even at its lowest state the murmuring of the falling water is distinctly heard. From the piazzas of the house, a long stretch of the summits of the Green Mountains are visible, although nowhere. nearer than twenty miles. Lake Champlain, from Burlington to Canada is seen, and far across the lake the Adirondacks lift their heads, while the spires of Montreal may be plainly distinguished towards the north. The pure mountain air of this region, laden with the balsamic odors from the many pine and hemlock trees which grow far and wide on either bank of the river, makes Congress Hall a resort especially adapted for persons threatened with throat or lung diseases. Sufferers from Hay Fever, who have lived at the seaside many seasons without permanent benefit, find certain relief here. Returning to St. Albans we pursue our journey northward.

Highgate Springs.—The springs at this station are within

a few rods of the railway, and one is tempted to try and taste the waters while the train is waiting. The Franklin House is an excellent hotel, and the vicinity of the springs makes it a very pleasant resort, many city visitors coming here for the summer. Missisquoi Bay (so named by the Indians, signifying "much water-fowl") is here about two miles wide, and teems with finny tribes throughout its entire length of thirty miles. Pickerel, black bass and muskalonge abound. In the late summer the bay swarms with ducks and

MISSISQUOI.

other water-fowl. Good boats and experienced boatmen are to be had at all times.

Off for Montreal.—Soon after leaving Highgate Springs the scenery ceases to become notably beautiful, although it is not destitute of interest, and occasionally a pretty stretch of country repays the watchful traveler. Entering the Victoria Bridge, but little can be seen excepting iron plates and braces, until after the space of six or ten minutes the train emerges from the western end of the bridge, and, following a descending grade, soon reaches the level of the streets, and in a

FRANKLIN HOUSE
LAPORTE, 1843-1888

few minutes enters the Montreal Depot. The Victoria Bridge is nearly two miles long. It is built on the tubular plan, and rests on two abutments and twenty-four piers. It cost $6,300,000.

A delightful excursion may be made by going to Montreal over a longer and more delightful route. Instead of proceeding to St. Johns, and over the Victoria Bridge, we go via the Ogdensburg & Lake Champlain Railroad. The first village we come to is

Swanton, a pleasant village of upwards of two thousand inhabitants, situated near the Missisquoi River, which supplies water-power for several woodenware factories.

874 MILES FROM BOSTON.
340 MILES FROM NEW YORK.
61 MILES FROM MONTREAL.

Alburgh Springs are on a peninsula between Missisquoi Bay and Lake Champlain, near the outlet of the latter. There is a large hotel at this place, and the renowned Lithia Springs, which attract large numbers of visitors from all parts of the country. Extensive accommodations are provided for hot and cold mineral baths. There are also pleasant drives, good fishing, and charming lake scenery in all directions. Seven miles farther west is

881 MILES FROM BOSTON.
347 MILES FROM NEW YORK.
67 MILES FROM MONTREAL.

Rouse's Point, situated at the north end of the lake, and commanding many fine views, embracing numerous islands and points of land. A very commodious hotel, the Windsor, has recently been built here near the lake shore, and the opportunities afforded for fishing, yachting, and driving has made this place one of the most attractive resorts in northern New York.

788 MILES FROM BOSTON.
361 MILES FROM NEW YORK.
68 MILES FROM MONTREAL.

Ottawa, the capital of the Dominion of Canada, may be reached from Rouse's Point by a short ride over the Canada Atlantic Railway. Passing through one of the richest agricultural districts in Canada, a rapid ride brings us to Valleyfield, a prosperous manufacturing town on the St. Lawrence River, at the head of the Coteau Rapids. Crossing the Beauharnois Canal, on an iron bridge, we skirt the shores of Clark's Island for a short distance, reaching the wharf on the north side of the island, and are conveyed across the river to Coteau by the powerful transfer steamer of the Canada Atlantic Railway. Continuing west, through pungent pine forests, interspersed by stretches of cultivated fields, we pass Eastman's

Springs, which are rapidly growing in popular favor, and the rivals of the famous Caledonia Springs. Eleven miles beyond, we cross the Rideau Canal and reach the banks of "Utawa's tide."

Ottawa is second to no city in Canada in natural charms, and is becoming every day more important as the capital of the great territory of British North America, now organized under the Government of the Dominion of Canada. In 1866 the British North American Act established the constitution of Canada in its present form, and fixed the capital permanently at Ottawa. The

PARLIAMENT BUILDINGS, OTTAWA.

Government Buildings at that city, begun in 1860, for Upper and Lower Canada, were utilized for the new Government, and with the additions and improvements, together with the grounds, have cost $5,000,000. There are three of them, forming a national monument of which Canadians may well be proud. Each of them is a magnificent pile, the centre building in particular, being one of the finest, outside and in, on this continent. The style of architecture is Gothic, of the 12th century, with some modifications to suit the climate. The materials are a cream-colored sandstone, with arches

of red sandstone, from Potsdam. The Senate Chamber, in which is
the throne occupied at the opening of the session by the Vice-Regal
Representative of Her Majesty, and the Hall of the House of Com-
mons, besides their great beauty, furnish an instructive and interesting lesson, on account of their close resemblance to the English
arrangements. The Library, in a unique and exquisite building at-
tached to this structure, is of great value and importance, and contains 200,000 volumes. The Post Office, the churches, the Dufferin
and Sapper's bridges, and the City Hall also ornament and beautify
the city, and enhance the work of nature in this favored spot. The
city stands on a plateau of horizontally stratified rocks, which rise
one hundred feet precipitously from the river. The scenery in every
direction from the city is grand and impressive. The Ottawa
River trends west in a dark blue line, its shore lined with dense
pine forests, the Laurentide Mountains rising from its banks and
stretching away to the north until their craggy heights are lost in the
hazy distance. To the east the roar of Chandiere Falls rises deep
and sullen above the din and noise of the many mills which crowd
the river's banks. Southward, the Rideau Canal cuts through the
city, while westward a pleasing landscape greets the eye. The Chandiere Falls, two hundred feet wide and forty deep, are excelled only
by Niagara, and furnish unlimited power for manufacturing purposes.
Ottawa has a population of about 40,000, and is the centre of an
enormous lumber trade. The hotels are good, the Russell House
being one of the finest in Canada.

As we pass west from Rouse's Point, over the Ogdensburg &
Lake Champlain Railroad, space permits mention of a few places
only : Champlain, on the Great Chazy River, has good water-power
and navigation to Lake Champlain, to which it chiefly owes its
prosperity. Chateaugay is an interesting place, from its extended
views, its proximity to Chateaugay Lake—the source of the river of
the same name—and that portion of the North Woods known as
the Chateaugay Woods. There are also very interesting springs,
falls, and picturesque scenery near, including the wonderful

Chateaugay Chasm, which bids fair to outrival Watkin's
Glen and Ausable Chasm ; it is located only two miles from the

CHATEAUGAY CHASM.

station, and well repays a visit. The stream has for centuries been wearing its way into the soft sandstone, assisted by the ice and frost, and now it has cut through the solid rock, making a chasm some 200 feet deep and not over thirty feet wide. A view of the chasm by moonlight is most impressive. The moon shines down on the walls of the chasm on one side, and on the water of the falls, while the other wall stands in shadow. In the spray dashed up from the cascade a lunar rainbow is formed. The perfect silence, except the roar of the falls, the bright moon shining on the water, the green ferns, vines and foliage on the rocks, and the rocks themselves, towering above, form one of the grandest and most beautiful of Nature's paintings. A good hotel has recently been built within a few rods of the entrance to the chasm.

Malone is the county town of Franklin County, on the Salmon River. It has beautiful streets and handsome public and private buildings. The Franklin Academy is here. The railroad depot is a large and handsome brick structure, and the hotel is fine and well kept. Meacham Lake and hunting-grounds are easily reached from Malone.

Moira, fifteen miles farther west, is the junction of the Northern Adirondack Railroad, recently constructed, and reaching into the heart of the Great Adirondack Wilderness. The road runs southeast through Dickinson, St. Regis Falls, Santa Clara, and Spring Cove to Paul Smith's Station, only seven miles from the noted resort bearing the same name, to which daily stages are run.

Paul Smith's stands on the north side of the Lower St. Regis Lake. The veteran proprietor came here in 1861, and built a small house among the pines for the accommodation of sportsmen ; but his enterprise gave him a rapid growth in business, until it has reached its present remarkable proportions. The present house is four stories high, luxuriously furnished, many rooms being *en suite*, and accommodates nearly 300 guests. A facetious writer has said that "Paul Smith's is a surprise to everybody ; an astonishing mixture of fish and fashion, pianos and puppies, Brussels carpeting and cowhide boots. Surrounded by a dense forest ; out of the way of all travel save that which is its own ; near the best hunting and

fishing grounds ; a first-class watering-place hotel, with all the modern
appliances, and a table that is seldom equaled in the best of city
hotels, set right down in the midst of a 'howling wilderness.'
Around the house the timid deer roam ; within, they rest. Out on
the lake the theoretical veteran casts all manner of flies ; in the
parlors the contents of huge Saratoga trunks are scientifically played,
and nets are spread for a different kind of fish. Poodles and
pointers, hounds, setters, dandies, and others of the species are found.
Feathers and fishing rods, point lace and pint bottles ; embryo Nim-
rods—who never knew a more destructive weapon than a yard-stick—
hung all around with revolvers and game-bags and cartridge-pouches
and sporting guns that are fearfully and wonderfully made, and which
would take a first-class engineer to work ; for you must know that
here danger is to be faced, that even the ladies bare arms, and are
said at such times to be very dangerous sportsmen indeed."

A telegraph line has been brought into this wilderness for the
express use of this house. The Lower St. Regis Lake is about two
miles long by one broad, and discharges west through the middle
branch of the St. Regis River. It is about 1600 feet above tide, and
the surrounding country is diversified by a multitude of small lakes
and ponds. St. Regis Mountain, toward the west, the ascent of
which constitutes a very pleasant day's excursion from the hotel,
yields a remarkably fine sight, upward of fifty distinct lakes and
ponds being visible. Prospect House on Upper Saranac Lake, and
Saranac Lake House on the Lower Lake, are reached from this
place by daily stages, Whiteface being east, and Ampersand, Seward,
Marcy, and a host of others lying toward the southwest from these
lakes.

Brasher Falls is the station nearest to Massena Springs, five
miles distant, to which stages run from Dunton's Hotel twice daily,
Sundays excepted, during the pleasure season. Massena Springs is a
popular resort. The water is sulphurous in character, and possesses
valuable medicinal properties. The village is neat, and in the season
of pleasure travel is gay and lively with guests. There are several
springs, of which St. Regis is the chief. At

Norwood the Potsdam branch of the Rome, Watertown &

Ogdensburg Railroad diverges for Rome and all points south and west. Potsdam is four miles south of the junction.

Ogdensburg, on the St. Lawrence River, at the mouth of the Oswegatchie River, is a town of about twelve thousand inhabitants, a United States port of entry and delivery, and a town of great commercial importance. It is handsomely laid out on a hillside and plateau, just at the mouth of the Oswegatchie, whose waters drive the machinery of its factories and mills. Its custom-house and post-office, built of Ohio sandstone at a cost of $200,000, is a fine structure. The city has many fine private residences along the east bank of the Oswegatchie. The main street is lined with well-built stores, banks, and public buildings. The business of the place is large. A steam ferry connects the city

TWIN BRIDGES, WINOUSKI

with Prescott, on the opposite shore of the River St. Lawrence, and with the Grand Trunk Railroad and the St. Lawrence & Ottawa Railway. Steamers of the Richelieu & Ontario Navigation Company run up the St. Lawrence to the Thousand Islands, Clayton and Toronto, and down the rapids of the St. Lawrence to Montreal and Quebec, connecting with the Ogdensburg & Lake Champlain, and the Rome, Watertown & Ogdensburg Railroads, and with trains of the Utica & Black River Railroad for Watertown, Lowville, Trenton Falls, Utica, etc.

After our run down the rapids of the St. Lawrence to Montreal we retrace our steps over the Central Vermont. Instead of returning by the route traveled on the outward journey, let us branch off at Essex Junction, and, using the Central Vermont's Rutland Division, take a hasty glance at another chain of the Green Hills. A few minutes' ride from Essex Junction brings us in view of the famous Winooski Gorge, which may be partially seen on our left, but bursts into full view as we shoot out upon the first of the two bridges by which it is spanned. The scenery is exceedingly wild and picturesque; the walls of the Gorge are three hundred feet apart and about one hundred high, and are cut into many fantastic forms and shapes by the erasive action of the turbulent river.

Winooski is a prosperous manufacturing village. Winooski Falls have some celebrity as one of the curiosities of the neighborhood, and are often visited by tourists stopping at Burlington. South of Winooski, on a hill, may be seen the granite column which stands over the grave of Ethan Allan.

Burlington was incorporated a city in 1866. It is delightfully situated on a hill, which rises from the shores of Lake Champlain, and commands a wide view of water and landscape. It is now the third lumber mart in the country, and the business is constantly increasing, large quantities being brought from Canada and the Lake shores, and shipped by rail to various markets. In the centre of the city is a large public square containing a fountain and shade trees. Near by are the Custom-House, City and County

Buildings, banks, and other business offices. The Van Ness and American Houses, on the southwest corner of the square, are reputed to be the most convenient and thoroughly appointed houses in Vermont. They contain very commodious sleeping rooms, with private parlors and other modern conveniences. The views from the hotel are rich and charming.

The University of Vermont stands on the crest of the hill overlooking the city. From the dome of the chief building an extensive and very beautiful view may be obtained, including the ranges of the Adirondack and Green Mountains, while Lake Champlain, with its bays and islands, stretches north and south as far as the eye can reach. The large island in front of Burlington is Juniper Island. To the south of this may be seen Rock Dunder, which is said to have excited the suspicions of the British Commodore, while cruising here during the war with England, to such an extent that he opened fire upon it. Colonel Ethan Allen, the gallant Vermonter, who, with his Green Mountain boys, rendered such service during the Revolution, was often in Burlington while living, and now lies in the Green Mountain Cemetery, near the city, where a granite monument has been erected by the State to perpetuate his memory. The scene, late in the afternoon, when the shifting hues of the sunset sky, and the more varied hues of the lake below, as orange changes to gold, and gold to crimson, and crimson to purple, and this to brown and dark gray and blue—all colors so shaded and intermingled that none can

be said to prevail alone—presents a view full of delight to the lover of nature.

In the country surrounding the city there are many romantic drives and walks; those leading along the Winooski River and to Shelburne Point and Harbor are, perhaps, the most attractive. Mallett's Bay, eight miles distant, is a beautiful sheet of water. One may also take the steamers across Lake Champlain to Port Kent (Ausable Chasm), Plattsburgh and the Adirondacks.

Lake Champlain.—Few lakes in the country possess so many claims upon the attention of the great public as does "the Gate of the Country," as it has been poetically designated by the early tribes of Indians who lived on its shores. Before the Dutch had commenced their settlements upon

Ruins of Old Fort Ticonderoga.

LAKE CHAMPLAIN and the Adirondacks, from the cupola of the Van Ness,
WILLIAMSTON, VT.

the Island of Manhattan, or Hendrick Hudson had discovered the noble river which bears his name; before the Mayflower, with her cargo of Puritans, had landed at Plymouth, the western borders of Vermont had been discovered and the waters of Lake Champlain had been explored by Samuel de Champlain. It is about 125 miles long, and varies from a few rods to thirteen miles in width. This channel thus opened formed the great highway between the Algonquins and Iroquois, as well as for the French and English, between Montreal and Fort Orange (Albany), and for a century and a half after became the theatre of the most savage and cruel wars between the Indian tribes; and some of the most bloody battles recorded in American history, between the French and English, were waged near these waters, long before the struggle of the Colonies for their independence had commenced. It was also the scene of several engagements during the war of 1812, the most important being the battle of Plattsburg, which was fought September 11th, 1814. The scenery is grand and peaceful, and to the disciple of old Izaak Walton it probably possesses more attractions than any other lake in the country. Its waters fairly teem with black bass, pickerel, pike, perch, and other families of the finny tribe.

Leaving Burlington by rail, charming meadow and mountain views from the east side of the cars are worthy the pencil of any artist, while on our right are the waters of the lake. Passing rapidly southward we reach

Vergennes, the oldest city in Vermont, and the smallest. It was incorporated a city in 1788, and is a little more than a mile square. It is situated on Otter Creek at the head of navigation. Vessels of 300 tons can lie almost alongside the bank anywhere below the city. It was here that Commodore McDonough's fleet fitted out during the war of 1812, and a United States arsenal is located here. At

913 MILES FROM BOSTON.
873 MILES FROM NEW YORK.
113 MILES FROM MONTREAL.

New Haven we can take the stage for Lincoln and Bristol, the latter a thriving town of about fifteen hundred inhabitants, five miles to the northeast. It is situated in the midst of a rich agricultural district, and is yearly growing in importance and wealth.

920 MILES FROM BOSTON.
875 MILES FROM NEW YORK.
102 MILES FROM MONTREAL.

Middlebury is pleasantly situated on the Otter River, and is
made famous by Middlebury College, erected
in 1800. The standard of the college, which is
in "Orthodox" hands, is very high. A little
farther southward, at

200 MILES FROM BOSTON.
244 MILES FROM NEW YORK.
136 MILES FROM MONTREAL.

Leicester Junction, the Addison division branches to the
west, crossing Lake Champlain by a bridge near
the ruins of Fort Ticonderoga. The village
of Ticonderoga is two miles from the station.
Stages leave the station on arrival of trains for Rogers' Rock Hotel,
on Lake George, six miles distant. From

195 MILES FROM BOSTON.
249 MILES FROM NEW YORK.
147 MILES FROM MONTREAL.

Brandon we take a stage for Lake Dunmore, one of the most
delightful resorts in the State. It is five miles
long, one mile wide, and covers a territory of
about fourteen hundred acres, at an altitude of
350 feet above the level of the sea. During the ride from Brandon we
are rewarded by many glimpses of charming woodland scenery. The
lake itself is second only to Lake George in picturesque beauty.
The western shores, where the hotel stands, are surrounded by undu-
lating meadows and wooded hills, while two or three spurs of the
Green Mountains rise to a height of fifteen hundred or two thousand
feet on the eastern side. These hills are accessible by pedestrians
or on horse-back, and from their summits extended views of the
surrounding country are obtainable. The pure mountain air, the
the restful shade of the groves, laden with resinous odors from the
pine and hemlock forests which grow far and near, and the peaceful
quiet which pervades the neighborhood have for many years made
this a favorite resort for many Boston, New York and Philadelphia
families.

183 MILES FROM BOSTON.
237 MILES FROM NEW YORK.
155 MILES FROM MONTREAL.

> " The balmiest sigh
> Which vernal zephyrs breathe in evening's ear,
> Were discord to the speaking quietude
> That wraps this moveless scene. Heaven's ebon vault,
> Studded with stars unutterably bright,
> Through which the moon's unclouded grandeur rolls
> Seems like a canopy which Love has spread
> To curtain her sleeping world. Yon gentle hills,
> Robed in a garment of unchanging green ;
> Yon darksome rocks, yon glittering stream :

LAKE DUNMORE

"All form a scene
Where musing solitude might love to lift
Her soul above this sphere of earthliness;
Where silence undisturbed might watch alone,
So clear, so bright, so still."

After leaving Brandon the country soon shows signs of those rich deposits of marble which have enriched this section of the State. Passing Pittsford, we find the first extensive quarries at

Sutherland Falls, where mills have been erected and many quarries are worked. The first marble quarry was opened at Dorset, in 1785, six years before the State was admitted into the Union.

173 MILES FROM BOSTON.
244 MILES FROM NEW YORK.
199 MILES FROM MONTREAL.

People came hundreds of miles to get the crude slabs for fire-place stones and other domestic uses. In 1808 a second quarry was opened, and subsequently many others, including those of Sutherland Falls, West Rutland and Centre Rutland. The channeling process, now familiar to mining engineers, was introduced in 1841; the first derrick for hoisting the blocks, in 1848; the first tunneling, in 1859. In 1818 the first attempt at sawing marble was made, but it was many years before the experiment proved successful. Of the town of

Rutland, some patriarch who should die now might say that he found it brick or frame and left it marble. The chaste, cold, and glossy stone is almost oppressively plenty in this busy, thriving village,

147 MILES FROM BOSTON.
233 MILES FROM NEW YORK.
171 MILES FROM MONTREAL.

and meets the eye in a multitude of forms and uses—buildings, pavements, walls—besides interior decoration and furnishing. Rutland is in fact its own best advertisement of its leading industry. To use the language of the exchange, its leading capitalists are already "in marble" before their death, and without the aid of the sculptor. To give an idea of the extent to which the marble interest engrosses the capacity and the resources of the neighborhood, we need only state that from fifteen to twenty quarries are being vigorously worked. The most important quarries and works are situated north and west of the town itself. Continuing our journey in a southeasterly direction and passing through the Clarendons (north and east), we pause a moment at

LUDLOW.

Cuttingsville to visit "Lucy's Cave." This cave is in one of the Shrewsbury Mountains. The entrance is near the top of the mountain, and is about four feet across, the cave descending almost

perpendicularly to an unknown depth. There is a legend regarding buried treasure connected with this cave, and some years ago, "Sleeping Lucy," in a trance, gave a vivid description of the place and its surroundings, saying she saw treasure in the shape of Spanish silver dollars. Search for the treasure has been made at different times, and many of the old residents still believe in her "prophecy." On we go, through East Wallingford and Mount Holly towards the summit of the western range of the Green Mountains. The scenery is varied, picturesque, lovely. The mountains close in gradually on either side as we mount higher and higher. Finally dashing through a rocky defile—where the road-bed has been cut through the solid rock which rise perpendicularly from fifty to one hundred—at an altitude of 1361 feet above the sea, we commence our descent towards Bellows Falls.

Ludlow, a neat, prosperous village on our left, is situated on the banks of the Black River, in a fertile val-

ley surrounded by high bleak hills, its pretty white houses, ornamented with green blinds, speaking of comfort and thrift, the village forms one of the fairest pictures in Vermont scenery. Another short run through Proctorsville, Cavendish, Gassetts, Chester and Bartonville, and we arrive at Bellows Falls, the terminus of the Central Vermont Railroad. Here connection is made via the Cheshire and Fitchburg Railroads for Boston.

Brattleboro & Whitehall Division.

THE Brattleboro and Whitehall Division extends from Brattleboro to South Londonderry, Vt., thirty-six miles. It is built along the bottom of a ravine in which there is barely room for the stream. The road, in many places, has been blasted out of the mountain side, and a fringe of trees, left at the water's edge, throw deep shadows across the bed of the West River, while, beyond the vista thus formed, many a bright bit of rustic scenery stands out in strong relief. It would be tedious to attempt to describe the beauties of this charming gorge, which in every rod of its devious ascent presents new and attractive features that bring forth some exclamation of surprise, admiration, or wonder. Long before the end of the road is reached our stock of expletives is exhausted; and, as we realize the beauty and extent of the scenes through which we have passed, silence seems the only way of expressing the rapture with which we are filled.

Not far distant is a spot known as the "Devil's Den." Climbing a ledge of bold, overhanging rocks, covered with the primeval forest, we look down into a chasm several hundred feet in depth, whence we see the tops of trees which have never heard the sound of woodman's axe; and thence up and away across a wide expanse of landscape, embracing extensive mountain ranges. It is indeed a wild and romantic spot.

A writer in *Outing* thus describes the view from the summit of one of the mountains near South Londonderry at an altitude of nearly 3000 feet above the sea level:

"If one can imagine himself upon the top of an immense wave in mid-ocean, surrounded on all sides by the swelling forms of

View from Glebe Mount.

Mill at So. Londonderry.

Near Plumley's Mills.

storm-vexed billows—and if those forms could be suddenly congealed
or rendered motionless—he would have an adequate conception of
the scene upon which our trio admiringly gazed. Away off to the
north the range, upon one of the spurs of which they stood,
trended away in ever changing and varied shapes, until the more
distant peaks melted tenderly into the cool grays of the clouds, and
it became a matter of discussion which was vapor and which solid
earth. To the east the undulations were less abrupt, but the eye
wandered over the contour of the billowy ranges, resting at last
upon the far distant horizon, where the peaks of the White Mountains cut the sky-line and stood plainly relieved against the azure of
the heaven above. Looking southward, the landscape gradually
assumed a more pastoral appearance, the extreme distance being
bounded by the Holyoke range, sixty miles away ; while, westward,
the Green Mountains surged and swelled in rocky waves, peak rising
above peak, range above range, culminating against the shadowy
Adirondacks, whose rugged outlines alone separated them from the
blue ether about them. The middle distance in each view was
made up of

> ' Hills rock-ribbed and ancient as the sun,
> With vales stretching in pensive quietness between
> Venerable woods—rivers that
> Moved in majesty, and complaining brooks
> That made the meadows green,'

with here and there the bright sheen of a silver lake, the taper
spire of a village church, or the lazily ascending smoke of a rustic
factory."

In concluding this hasty record of a trip among the Green
Mountain By-Ways, I would only add that to the angler, or the
man or woman seeking after rest and retirement from the bustle,
confusion and fashion of the city, the Central Vermont Railroad
offers superior inducements. Excellent fishing, quiet, peaceful re-
pose, delightful scenery, healthful food, bracing, stimulating air—in
fact, every desideratum for a summer's vacation can be found along
the line of this Railroad, its leased lines, and its many connections.
In respect to diversity and beauty of scenery, this road is unex-
celled by any in this country.

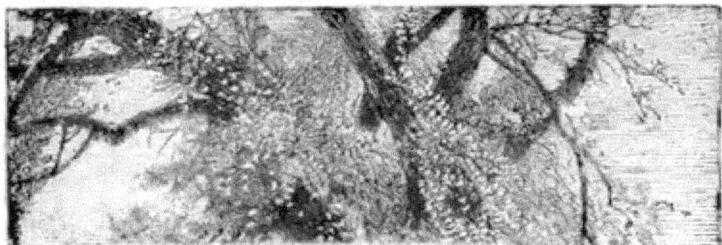

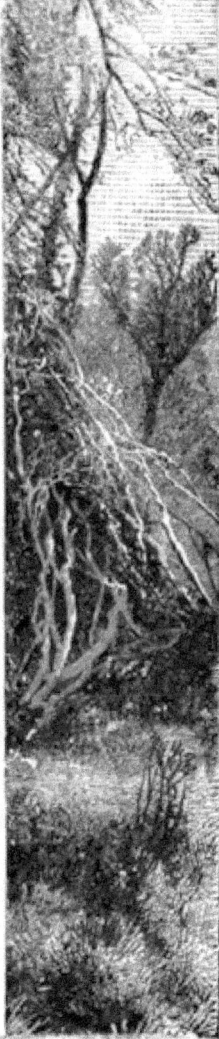

FISH AND GAME LAWS

OF VERMONT.

The following is a synopsis of the Game and Fish Laws of Vermont.

Game may be killed in Vermont only during the seasons stated below :

GAME.

It is unlawful to take or kill a wild deer within the State prior to the ·st of November, 1890.

Mink, Beaver, Fisher, or Otter, between November 1st and April 1st following ; Woodcock, Quail, or Ruffled Grouse (partridge), between September 1st and February 1st following ; Wild Ducks and Geese, between September 1st and May 1st. Persons who shall at any time take or destroy the eggs of any of the above-named birds, or take such birds by means of a snare, net, or trap, are liable to a fine of ten dollars. It is unlawful to shoot or destroy a Robin, Blue-bird, Yellow-bird, Cherry or Cedar bird, Cat-bird, King-bird, Sparrow (English Sparrows not included), Lark, Bobolink, Thrush, Chickadee, Peewee, Wren, Warbler, Martin, Swallow, Night-hawk, Whip-poor-will, Ground-bird, Linnet, Plover, Tattler, Phœbe, Creeper, Bunting, or Humming-bird, or destroy the eggs or nests of such birds.

FISH.

Black Bass, Wall-eyed Pike, or Pike Perch may be caught between June 15th and February 1st following ; Trout, Land-locked Salmon, Salmon-trout, or Longe, between May 1st and September 1st following ; White-fish, or Lake Shad, between November 15th and November 1st following. The law further provides that Black Bass less than ten inches long shall be at once returned to the water and set free therein. Fishing with pound-net, trap-net, set-net or device other than hook and line, or angling, is unlawful.

STRAY NOTES

Flora, Geology and Mineralogy

OF VERMONT.

— — · —

BOTANY.

A FEW OF THE PLANTS FOUND IN VERMONT.

— · —

" The fields, meadows, and groves of Vermont afford a flora of very great richness and beauty, interesting to every one who loves flowers and plants, but especially so to the scientific botanist, who not only admires the outward form and beauty of a plant, but derives a deeper joy from an investigation of its mode of growth, structure, and economy."

BOTANICAL NAMES.	COMMON NAME.	WHERE FOUND.
Abutilon Avicenæ	Velvet Leaf	Common in waste places.
Acorus Calamus	Sweet Flag	Common on margins of rivulets and in swamps.
Adiantum pedatum	Maiden-hair Fern	Common in damp woods.
Adlumia cirrhosa	Mountain Fringe	In rocky ravines—rare.
Ampelopsis quinquefolia	Woodbine	Common in woods.
Anemone	Wind-flower	
" cylindrica	Long-fruited flower	Sparingly in sandy or dry wood in many localities.
" multifida	Many-cleft flower	Common near Burlington.
" nemorosa	Wind-flower	Common in open woods and copses in southern Vermont
Aquilegia Canadensis	Columbine	Common on the rocks.
Astragalus Robbinsii		Found only at High Bridge, in the Winooski River.
Barbarea vulgaris	Winter Cress	Meadows and roadsides—rather common.
Betula papyracea	Paper or Canoe Birch	Common.
Calla palustris	Calla	Swamps—common.
Caltha "	Marsh Marigold	Common in wet meadows and swamps.
Calypso borealis	Calypso	In swamps—very rare.
Campanula	Harebell	
" rotundifolia		Rocky, shaded banks—common.
" rapunculoides		Brandon.
Camptosorus rhizophyllus	Walking Fern	Common.
Carya alba	Walnut	Most common near Lake Champlain.
Castilleia pallida	Painted Cup	North side of Mt. Mansfield.
Celastrus scandens	Climbing Bittersweet	Common along streams and in thickets.
Clematis	Virgin's Bower	
" verticillaris		Rocky places in mountains.

BOTANY—Continued.

BOTANICAL NAMES.	COMMON NAMES.	WHERE FOUND.
Clematis viorna		Castleton, near Brattleboro.
" Virginiana		Common in damp thickets.
Comptonia asplenifolia	Sweet Fern	Common on dry soil.
Coptis trifolia	Goldthread	Common in clearings and edges of groves.
Epigæa repens	Trailing Arbutus, Mayflower	Common in sandy woods, and sometimes on rocky soil, especially in the shade of pines.
Euonymus atropurpureus	Burning Bush	Found wild in some parts of the State.
Gaultheria, procumbens	Creeping Wintergreen	Common in cold, damp woods, most in shade of evergreens.
Gentiana crinita	Fringed Gentian	Damp meadows.
" amarella		Smuggler's Notch.
Geranium maculatum	Cranesbill	Common.
" dissectum	Cut-leaved Cranesbill	Hills near Castleton.
Gerardia flava	Foxglove	Open woods in southern part of State.
Hedeoma pulegioides	Pennyroyal	Common in dry fields.
Hudsonia tomentosa	Hudsonia	Colchester Point.
Houstonia cærulea	Forget-me-nots	Common.
Iris, versicolor	Blue Flag	Common.
Juglans, cinerea	Butternut	Common over entire State.
Liriodendron tulipifera	Tulip Tree, White Wood	Southern part of State.
Leucanthemum vulgare	Daisy	Very common.
Linum Virginianum	Flax	Dry woods, Pownal.
Lonicera parviflora	Honeysuckle	Rocks on shores of Lake Champlain.
" cærulea	"	Mountains and swamps.
Lupinus perennis	Lupine	Common on sandy soil.
Lycopodium Selago	Ground Pine	Mountain summits.
" innundatum	" "	Sterling Pond.
" dendroideum	" "	Woods.
Mentha viridis	Spearmint	Common in wet places.
" piperita	Peppermint	On low ground and along banks.
Melilotus alba	Sweet Clover	Common.
Medicago lupulina	Black Medick	So. Hero—rare.
Monarda fistulosa	Wild Bergamot	Dry woods—rare.
Nuphar advena	Yellow Pond-lily	Common in still or stagnant water.
" pumilum	" " "	Lake Champlain, near Burlington.
Nymphæa odorata	Water-lily	Common.
" tuberosa	" "	Mouth of Missisquoi River, Winooski River.
Œnothera fruticosa	Evening Primrose	Willoughby Lake.
Onoclea sensibilis	Sensitive Fern	Common.
Osmorhiza longistylis	Sweet Cicely	Rich woods.
Phlox subulata	Moss Pink	Mt. Mansfield.
Polanisia graveolens	Polanisia	Gravelly shores of Lake Champlain.
Primula Mistassinica	Primrose	Willoughby Mountains.
Rhus typhina	Staghorn Sumach	Hillsides—common.
" Toxicodendron	Poison Ivy	Common.
Rosa lucida	Dwarf Wild Rose	Shores of Lake Champlain—rare.
" rubiginosa	Sweet Brier	Rocky pastures—rare.
Sanguinaria Canadensis	Blood Root	Open, rich woods.
Sarracenia purpurea	Pitcher Plant	Common in swamps.
Saxifraga aizoides	Yellow Saxifrage	Mt. Mansfield, Willoughby Lake.
Sedum acre	Live-for-ever	Norwich, on rocks.
Silene noctiflora	Night-flowering Catchfly	Common.
Solidago Canadensis	Golden Rod	Along fences and edges of woods.
" Muhlenbergii	" "	Brattleboro.
" rigida	" "	Burlington.
" thrysoides	" "	Willoughby and Mansfield Mountains.
Symphoricarpus racemosus	Snow Berry	Rocky shores of Lake Champlain and some of the islands.
Trillium grandiflorum	Large White Trillium	Abundant in Western Vermont.
" cernuum	Nodding Trillium	Southern part of State.
Typha latifolia	Cat-tail Flag	Swamps—common.
" angustifolia		Ferrisburgh.
Viola, blanda	Sweet White Violet	Wet meadows and woods—common.
" Selkirkii	Great-spurred Violets	Cedar swamps—rare.
" pedata	Bird-foot Violets	Brattleboro.
Vitis riparia	Frost Grape	Thickets, river banks.
Woodwardia Virginica	Chair Fern	Colchester Pond, swamps.
Xanthoxylum Americanum	Prickly Ash	Middlebury, Ferrisburgh, Grand Isle, St. Albans.

GEOLOGY AND MINERALOGY.

MINERALS.	WHERE FOUND.
Actynolite	Windham, Grafton, Newfane, Brattleboro.
Aluminous Slate	Pownal, Rockingham.
Amethyst	Westminster, Ludlow.
Argillaceous Slate:	
Black	Northfield, along Connecticut River.
Purple and Green	Castleton, Fairhaven, Poultney.
Asbestos	Mount Holly, Lowell, Troy.
Bitter Spar	Grafton, Bridgewater.
Blende	Orwell.
Calcareous Spar	Vergennes, Shoreham.
Chalcedony	Newfane.
Chlorite	Grafton, Bethel.
Copper	Vershire, Corinth.
Cyanite	Grafton, Bellows Falls.
Dolomite	Jamaica.
Feldspar	Townshend, Thetford, Monkton.
Garnet	Bethel, Norwich.
Granite	Rare in Western Vermont, abundant in Eastern Vermont, quarried at Barre, Derby, Victory.
Graphite	Hancock, Charlotte.
Hornblende	Jericho, Ludlow.
Hornstone	Middlebury, Shoreham, Bennington.
Iron	Bennington, Plymouth.
Jasper	Middlebury.
Kaolin	Monkton, Brookline.
Lithomarge	Bennington.
Marble :	
White	Rutland, Dorset, Pittsford, Middlebury.
White statuary	Brandon.
Clouded	Sutherland Falls, East Dorset.
Variegated	Colchester.
Dove-colored	Swanton.
Dark	Isle La Motte.
Marl	Peacham, Barnard, Alburgh.
Mica	Chester, Craftsbury, Orange.
Potter's Clay	Middlebury.
Prehnite	Bellows Falls.
Quartz :	
Greasy	Grafton, New Haven.
Crystal	Castleton, Waitsfield, St. Johnsbury.
Milky	Stockbridge, Grafton.
Smoky	Shrewsbury.
Steatite or Soapstone	Windsor County,
Stalactite	Bennington, Dorset, Montpelier.
Sulphur	Wilmington, Bridgewater.
Tourmaline	Peacham.
Zinc	Orwell.

FOSSILS.

FOSSILS	WHERE FOUND.
Maclurea magna	Chazy Limestone—Found at McNeill's Point, Charlotte, Grand Isle and Isle La Motte, also Addison, Panton.
Orthoceras vertebrale	Bridport, Larrabee's Point.
Columnaria alveolata	" " "
Asaphus gigas	" " "
Chaetetes lycoperdon	" " "
Orthis testudinaria	" " "
Rhynchonella plena	McNeill's Point.
Pleurotomaria calcifera	" "
Leptaena sericea	" " Isle La Motte, Addison, etc.
Lingula quadrata	Addison.
Graptolithus pristis	Ladds, Grand Isle.
Carpolithes Brandonensis	Brandon.
Macoma fusca	Burlington.
Saxicava rugosa	"

SPECIAL LIMITED EXCURSIONS TO VERMONT

Special Excursion No. 1.

Via CONCORD and WHITE RIVER JUNCTION.

Boston to Nashua ....Boston & Maine R. R.
Nashua to Concord ....Concord R. R.
Concord to White River Junction........Boston & Maine R. R.
White River Junction to following stations. Central Vermont R. R.
Return same Route.

Sharon	$7 40	Essex Junction	11 00
So. Royalton	7 70	Burlington	11 00
Bethel	8 20	Milton	11 50
Randolph	8 70	Georgia	11 75
Roxbury	9 00	St. Albans	12 00
Northfield	9 25	Swanton	12 50
Montpelier	9 50	Alburgh Springs	12 50
Barre	10 00	Rouse's Point	13 00
Waterbury	10 00	Highgate Springs	12 50
Richmond	10 75	St. Johns	14 50

Special Excursion No. 2.

Via BELLOWS FALLS and RUTLAND.

Boston to Fitchburg ....Fitchburg R. R.
Fitchburg to Bellows Falls................Cheshire R. R.
Bellows Falls to following points.........Central Vermont R. R.
Return same Route.

Chester	$7 50	Burlington	$11 00
Ludlow	8 00	Winooski	11 00
Cuttingsville	8 50	Essex Junction	11 00
Rutland	9 00	Milton	11 50
Pittsford	9 40	Georgia	11 75
Brandon	9 75	St. Albans	12 00
Ticonderoga	11 00	Swanton	12 50
Middlebury	10 50	Alburgh Springs	12 50
Vergennes	10 75	Rouse's Point	13 00
Charlotte	11 00	Highgate Springs	12 50
Shelburne	11 00	St. Johns	14 50

Excursion No. 3.

BOSTON to STOWE and return.

(MT. MANSFIELD.)

Boston to Nashua.......................Boston & Maine R. R.
Nashua to Concord ....Concord R. R.
Concord to White River Junction........Boston & Maine R. R.
White River Junction to Waterbury.......Central Vermont R. R.
Waterbury to Stowe....................Stage.

Return same Route.

RATE,   -   -   - $11.00

Carriages from Stowe to summit Mt. Mansfield, daily.

Excursion No. 3 a.

BOSTON to BURLINGTON and return.

Boston to Nashua.......................Boston & Maine R. R.
Nashua to Concord...,..................Concord R. R.
Concord to White River Junction........Boston & Maine R. R.
White River Junction to Burlington......Central Vermont R. R.

Return same Route.

RATE,   -   -   - $11.00

Excursion No. 3 b.

BOSTON to BURLINGTON and return.

Boston to Fitchburg....................Fitchburg R. R.
Fitchburg to Bellows Falls.............Cheshire R. R.
Bellows Falls to Burlington............Central Vermont R. R.

Return same Route.

RATE,   -   -   - $11.00

Excursion No. 4.

BOSTON to ST. ALBANS and return.

Boston to Nashua ....Boston & Maine R. R.
Nashua to Concord ....Concord R. R.
Concord to White River Junction ....Boston & Maine R. R.
White River Junction to St. Albans ......Central Vermont R. R.

Return same Route.

RATE,   -   -   - $12.00

LAKE CHAMPLAIN FROM ST. ALBANS

Excursion No. 5.

BOSTON to ST. ALBANS and return.

ROUTE GOING :

Boston to Fitchburg .... Fitchburg R. R.
Fitchburg to Bellows Falls............ Cheshire R. R.
Bellows Falls to St. Albans via Rutland ..Central Vermont R. R.

ROUTE RETURNING :

St. Albans to White River Junction ......Central Vermont R. R.
White River Junction to Concord........Boston & Maine R. R.
Concord to Nashua.....................Concord R. R.
Nashua to Boston ....Boston & Maine R. R.

RATE,   -   -   - $12.00

Excursion No. 6.

BOSTON to SHELDON SPRINGS and return.

Boston to Nashua.....................Boston & Maine R. R.
Nashua to Concord....................Concord R. R.
Concord to White River Junction ....Boston & Maine R. R.
White River Junction to St. Albans ......Central Vermont R. R.
St. Albans to Sheldon Springs ....Central Vermont R. R.
Return same Route.

RATE,   -   -   - $12.50

Excursion No. 7.

BOSTON to SHELDON SPRINGS and return.

Boston to Fitchburg ....Fitchburg R. R.
Fitchburg to Bellows Falls............. ..Cheshire R. R.
Bellows Falls to St. Albans via Rutland ⎫ Central Vermont R. R.
and Burlington................... ⎭
St. Albans to Sheldon Springs ....Central Vermont R. R.
Return same Route.

RATE,   -   -   - $12.50

Excursion No. 8.

BOSTON to ALBURGH SPRINGS and return.

Boston to Nashua.....................Boston & Maine R. R.
Nashua to Concord....................Concord R. R.
Concord to White River Junction........Boston & Maine R. R.
White River Junction to Alburgh Springs.Central Vermont R. R.
Return same Route.

RATE,   -   -   - $12.50

Excursion No. 9.

BOSTON to ALBURGH SPRINGS and return.

ROUTE GOING :

Boston to Fitchburg ....Fitchburg R. R.
Fitchburg to Bellows Falls ....Cheshire R. R.
Bellows Falls to Alburgh Springs, via } Central Vermont R. R.
   Rutland and Burlington...........

ROUTE RETURNING :

Alburgh Springs to White River Junction.Central Vermont R. R.
White River Junction to Concord........Boston & Maine R. R.
Concord to Nashua................. ....Concord R. R.
Nashua to Boston ....Boston & Maine R. R.

      RATE,   - - - $12.50

Excursion No. 10.

BOSTON to ALBURGH SPRINGS and return

A reverse of Excursion No. 9.

      RATE,   - - - $12.50

Excursion No. 11.

BOSTON to HIGHGATE SPRINGS and return.

Boston to Nashua . ...Boston & Maine R. R.
Nashua to Concord.....................Concord R. R.
Concord to White River Junction........Boston & Maine R. R.
White River Junction to Highgate Springs.Central Vermont R. R.
      Return same Route.

      RATE,   - - - $12.50

Excursion No. 12.

BOSTON to HIGHGATE SPRINGS and return.

ROUTE GOING :

Boston to Fitchburg .... Fitchburg R. R.
Fitchburg to Bellows Falls.............Cheshire R. R.
Bellows Falls to Highgate Springs, via } Central Vermont R. R.
   Rutland and Burlington...........

ROUTE RETURNING :

Highgate Springs to White River Junction.Central Vermont R. R.
White River Junction to Concord........Boston & Maine R. R.
Concord to Nashua.....................Concord R. R.
Nashua to Boston ....Boston & Maine R. R.

      RATE,   - - - $12.50

Excursion No. 13.

BOSTON to HIGHGATE SPRINGS and return.

A Reverse of Excursion No.12.

RATE, - - $12.50

Excursion No. 14.

BOSTON to ALBURGH or HIGHGATE SPRINGS and return.

ROUTE GOING :

Boston to Alburgh or Highgate Springs...Via White River June. or Rutland.

ROUTE RETURNING :

Alburgh or Highgate Springs to Montpelier.Central Vermont R. R.
Montpelier to Well's River ....Montpelier & Wells River R. R.
Well's River to Fabyan's ....Boston & Lowell R. R. (W. M. Div.)
Fabyan's to N. Conway via Notch.......Maine Central R. R.
North Conway to Boston ....Boston & Maine R. R.

Or *vice versa.*

RATE, - - - $18.00

Excursion No. 15.

BOSTON to CHATEAUGAY CHASM and return.

Boston to Rouse's Point ....Via White River June. or Rutland.
Rouse's Point to Chateaugay ....Central V't R. R. (O. & L. C. Div.)
Chateaugay to Chasm..................Coach.

Return same Route.

RATE, - - - $15.00

Excursion No. 16.

BOSTON to SARATOGA SPRINGS and return.

Boston to Fitchburg....................Fitchburg R. R.
Fitchburg to Bellows Falls..............Cheshire R. R.
Bellows Falls to Rutland................Central Vermont R. R.
Rutland to Saratoga ....Del. & Hudson Canal Co's R. R.

Return same Route.

RATE, - - - $10.00

Excursion No. 17,

BOSTON to SARATOGA SPRINGS and return.

Boston to North Adams via Hoosac Tunnel.Fitchburg R. R.
North Adams to Saratoga...............Fitchburg R. R.

Return via Rutland and Bellows Falls.

RATE, - - - $10.00

LAKE CHAMPLAIN

Excursion No. 18.

BOSTON to SARATOGA and return.

Boston to Albany.................... ...Boston & Albany R. R.
Albany to Saratoga......................Del. & Hudson Canal Co's R. R.
Return via Rutland & Bellows Falls.
RATE,   -   -   - $10.00

Excursion. No. 19.

BOSTON to LAKE GEORGE and return.

ROUTE GOING :

Boston to Fitchburg.....................Fitchburg R. R.
Fitchburg to Bellows Falls...............Cheshire R. R.
Bellows Falls to Rutland......... ....Central Vermont R. R.
Rutland to Caldwell (Lake George) ....Del. & Hudson Canal Co's R. R.

ROUTE RETURNING :

Caldwell to Baldwin....................Lake George Steamers.
Baldwin to Rutland ....Del. & Hudson Canal Co's R. R.
Rutland to Bellows Falls.................Central Vermont R. R.
Bellows Falls to Fitchburg...............Cheshire R. R.
Fitchburg to Boston....................Fitchburg R. R.
RATE,   -   -   - $14.75

Excursion No. 20.

BOSTON to LAKE GEORGE and return.

A Reverse of Excursion No. 19.
RATE,   -   -   - $14.75

Excursion No. 21.

BOSTON to LAKE CHAMPLAIN and return.

ROUTE GOING :

Boston to Nashua.......................Boston & Maine R. R.
Nashua to Concord.....................Concord R. R.
Concord to White River Junction.........Boston & Maine R. R.
White River Junction to Burlington.......Central Vermont R. R.

ROUTE RETURNING :

Burlington to Fort Ticonderoga..........Lake Champlain Steamers.
Fort Ticonderoga to Rutland............Del. & Hudson Canal Co's R. R.
Rutland to Bellows Falls.................Central Vermont R. R.
Bellows Falls to Fitchburg..............Cheshire R. R.
Fitchburg to Boston....................Fitchburg R. R.
RATE,   -   -   - $14.30

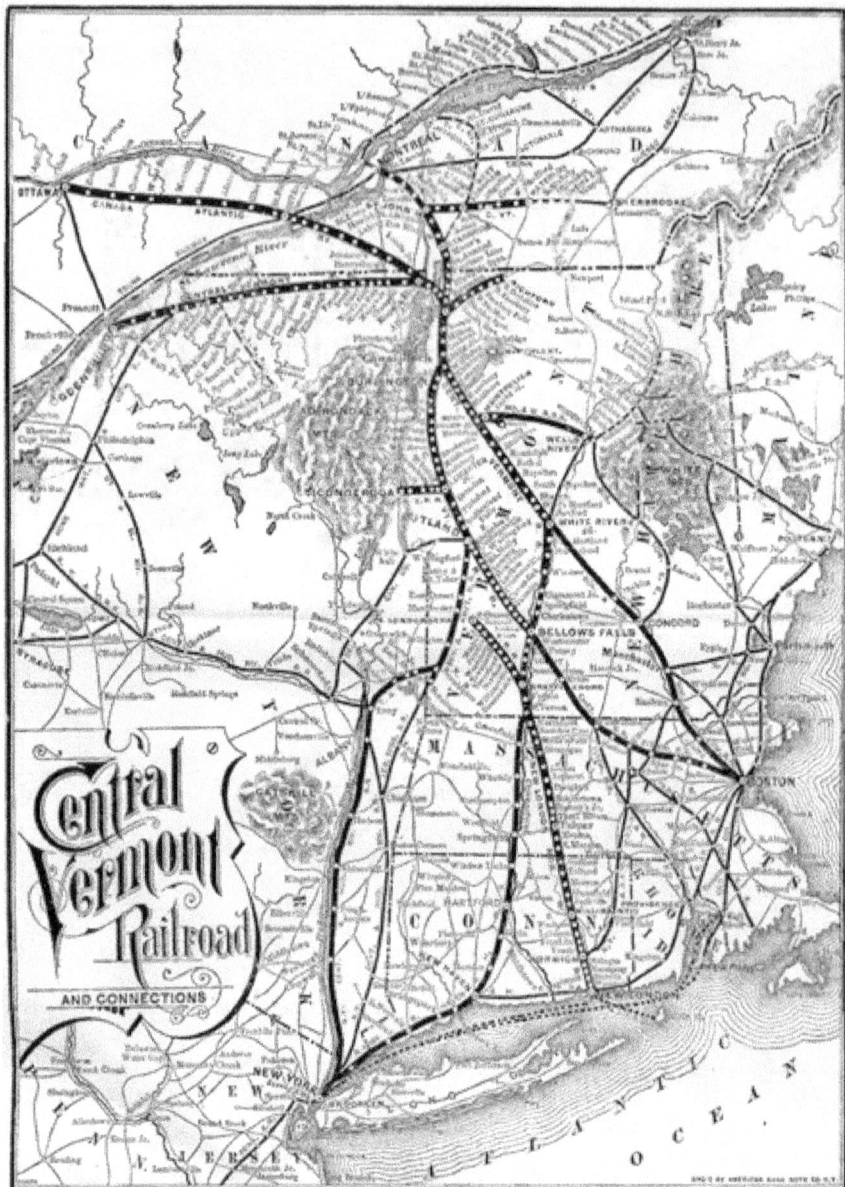

Central
Vermont
Railroad

AND CONNECTIONS

Excursion No. 22.

BOSTON to LAKE CHAMPLAIN and return.

A Reverse of Excursion No. 21.

RATE, · - $14.30

Excursion No. 23.

BOSTON to LAKES GEORGE, CHAMPLAIN and return.

ROUTE GOING :

Boston to Fitchburg	Fitchburg R. R.
Fitchburg to Bellows Falls	Cheshire R. R.
Bellows Falls to Rutland	Central Vermont R. R.
Rutland to Caldwell via Saratoga	Del. & Hudson Canal Co's R. R.

ROUTE RETURNING :

Caldwell to Baldwin	Lake George Steamers.
Baldwin to Ft. Ticonderoga	Del. & Hudson Canal Co's R. R
Fort Ticonderoga to Burlington	Lake Champlain Steamers.
Burlington to White River Junction	Central Vermont R. R.
White River Junction to Concord	Boston & Maine R. R
Concord to Nashua	Concord R. R.
Nashua to Boston	Boston & Maine R. R.

RATE, · · - $17.75

Excursion No. 24.

BOSTON to LAKES GEORGE, CHAMPLAIN and return.

A Reverse of Excursion No. 23.

RATE, · · - $17.75

Excursion No. 25.

BOSTON to SARATOGA and return.

ROUTE GOING :

Boston to Fitchburg	Fitchburg R. R.
Fitchburg to Bellows Falls	Cheshire R. R.
Bellows Falls to Rutland	Central Vermont R. R.
Rutland to Albany via Saratoga	Del. & Hudson Canal Co's R. R.

ROUTE RETURNING :

Albany to New York	Hudson River Steamers.
New York to Boston	Sound Lines Steamers.

RATE, · · - $12.35

Excursion No. 26.

BOSTON to SARATOGA and return.

A Reverse of Excursion No. 25.

RATE, · · - $12.35

BOSTON to BURLINGTON and return.

(LAKE CHAMPLAIN.)

ROUTE GOING :

Boston to New York ....Sound Line Steamers.
New York to Albany.................Hudson River Steamers.
Albany to Fort Ticonderoga via Saratoga...Del. & Hudson Canal Co's R. R.
Fort Ticonderoga to Burlington..........Lake Champlain Steamers.

ROUTE RETURNING :

Burlington to White River Junction.......Central Vermont R. R.
White River Junction to Concord........Boston & Maine R. R.
Concord to Nashua......... ....Concord R. R.
Nashua to Boston.....................Boston & Maine R. R.

RATE,   -   -   - $17.40

Excursion No. 28.

BOSTON to BURLINGTON and return.

A Reverse of Excursion No. 27.

RATE,   -   -   - $17.40

Excursion No. 29.

BOSTON to BURLINGTON and return.

ROUTE GOING :

Boston to Fitchburg.....................Fitchburg R. R.
Fitchburg to Bellows Falls ....Cheshire R. R.
Bellows Falls to Burlington via Rutland....Central Vermont R. R.

ROUTE RETURNING :

Burlington to Fort Ticonderoga..........Lake Champlain Steamers.
Fort Ticonderoga to Albany via Saratoga..Del. & Hudson Canal Co's R. R.
Albany to New York....................Hudson River Steamers.
New York to Boston ....Sound Lines Steamers.

RATE,   -   -   - $17.40

Excursion No. 30.

BOSTON to BURLINGTON and return.

A Reverse of Excursion No. 29.

RATE,   -   -   - $17.40

Excursion No. 31.

BOSTON to BURLINGTON and return.

(Lakes George and Champlain.)

ROUTE GOING :

Boston to Nashua........................Boston & Maine R. R.
Nashua to Concord......................Concord R. R.
Concord to White River Junction........Boston & Maine R. R.
White River Junction to Burlington......Central Vermont R. R.

ROUTE RETURNING :

Burlington to Fort Ticonderoga..........Lake Champlain Steamers.
Fort Ticonderoga to Baldwin.............Del. & Hudson Canal Co's R. R.
Baldwin to Caldwell.....................Lake George Steamers.
Caldwell to Albany via Saratoga.........Del. & Hudson Canal Co's R. R.
Albany to New York......................Hudson River Steamers.
New York to Boston......................Sound Lines Steamers.

RATE, - - - $19.40

Excursion No. 32.

BOSTON to BURLINGTON and return.

A Reverse of Excursion No. 31.

RATE, - - - $19.40

Excursion No. 33.

BOSTON to BURLINGTON and return.

ROUTE GOING :

Boston to New York.....................Sound Lines Steamers.
New York to Albany.....................Hudson River Steamers.
Albany to Caldwell via Saratoga........Del. & Hudson Canal Co's R. R.
Caldwell to Baldwin....................Lake George Steamers.
Baldwin to Fort Ticonderoga............Del. & Hudson Canal Co's R. R.
Fort Ticonderoga to Burlington.........Lake Champlain Steamers.

ROUTE RETURNING :

Burlington to Bellows Falls via Rutland...Central Vermont R. R.
Bellows Falls to Fitchburg..............Cheshire R. R.
Fitchburg to Boston.....................Fitchburg R. R.

RATE, - - - $19.40

Excursion No. 34.

BOSTON to BURLINGTON and return.

A Reverse of Excursion No. 33.

RATE, - - - $19.40

MONTREAL, the commercial metropolis of the Dominion of Canada, is situated on the south shore of an island bearing the same name, and at the base of a beautiful eminence known as Mount Royal. The site of the city was first visited by Jacques Cartier, in 1535. Champlain also visited it in 1611, but the first settlement was not formed until 1642, by M. de Maisonneuve. When Canada was conquered by the British in 1759, Montreal had population of 4,000 souls. Its present population is over 175,000.

The city is laid in the form of a parallelogram. It is built mostly of a grayish limestone from adjacent quarries, and with its handsome spires, glittering tin roofs, and the picturesque vales that stud its lofty background, is seen to great advantage from the river. The old part of Montreal near the river has narrow, incommodious streets, but the new growth of the city toward Mount Royal has been liberally laid out, with wide, cheerful thoroughfares. The architecture here is very fine.

Among places of interest may be mentioned the Parish Church of Notre Dame. The dimensions of this vast Norman edifice are 241 feet in length, and 135 feet in width. Two main towers in front rise 220 feet, the western tower, containing a peal of bells, one of which weighs upwards of 29,000 pounds, and is the largest bell in America. The seating capacity of the church is 10,000. It has recently been decorated in deep colors and gold, after the manner of the Sainte Chapelle at Paris. Christ Church Cathedral on St. Catherine's Street is undoubtedly the finest specimen of Gothic architecture in Canada. The Bank of Montreal, Post-office, City Hall, Bonsecour Market, Windsor Hotel, Church of the Gesu and many other churches, McGill College, etc., etc., are also worthy of mention.

The view from Mount Royal is delightful. Suddenly, after an easy ascent by a winding path, we are looking forth on the city with its spires, its gardens and avenues; beyond is the broad flowing St. Lawrence, with Victoria Bridge and the Lachine Rapids just visible in the distance; fading away toward the horizon are the hills of Vermont and the Adirondacks many miles away. The summit of the mount is very beautifully diversified with hillocks and dells; nearly every Canadian tree grows upon it, and ferns and wild flowers abound. Overhead flutter the robin, the catbird, and the bluebird; while the brilliant plumage of the oriole occasionally attracts the observer's attention. Other drives are around the Mountain; to Lachine; to Longue Point; and to the Back River.

Excursion No. 35.

BOSTON to MONTREAL and return.

Boston to Nashua ....Boston & Maine R. R.
Nashua to Concord ....Concord R. R.
Concord to White River Junction ....Boston & Maine R. R.
White River Junction to St. Johns.......Central Vermont R. R.
St. Johns to Montreal..................Grand Trunk R'y.
Return same Route.
RATE, - - - $16.00

Excursion No. 36.

BOSTON to MONTREAL and return.

Boston to Fitchburg....................Fitchburg R. R.
Fitchburg to Bellows Falls ....Cheshire R. R.
Bellows Falls to St. Johns via Rutland and Burlington...... ....} Central Vermont R. R.
St. Johns to Montreal and Return ....Grand Trunk R'y.
Return same Route.
RATE. - - $16.00

Excursion No. 37.

BOSTON to MONTREAL and return.

ROUTE GOING :

Boston to Nashua ....Boston & Maine R. R.
Nashua to Concord......................Concord R. R.
Concord to White River Junction.........Boston & Maine R. R.
White River Junction to St. Johns ....Central Vermont R. R.
St. Johns to Montreal and return ....Grand Trunk R'y.

ROUTE RETURNING :

Montreal to St. Johns....................Grand Trunk R'y.
St. Johns to Bellows Falls via Burlington } Central Vermont R. R.
    and Rutland......................
Bellows Falls to Fitchburg ....Cheshire R. R.
Fitchburg to Boston ....Fitchburg R. R.
RATE,   -   -   - $16.00

Excursion No. 38.

BOSTON to MONTREAL and return.

A Reverse of Excursion No. 37.
RATE,   -   -   - $16.00

Excursion No. 39.

BOSTON to MONTREAL and return.

ROUTE GOING :

Boston to Nashua........................Boston & Maine R. R.
Nashua to Concord ....Concord R. R.
Concord to Wells River.................Boston & Maine R. R.
Wells River to Newport.................Boston & Maine R. R.
Newport to Montreal....................Canadian Pacific R'y.

ROUTE RETURNING :

Montreal to St. Johns....................Grand Trunk Railway.
St. Johns to White River Junction.......Central Vermont R. R.
White River Junction to Concord.........Boston & Maine R. R.
Concord to Nashua.....................Concord R. R.
Nashua to Boston......................Boston & Maine R. R.
RATE,   -   -   - $16.00

Excursion No. 40.

BOSTON to MONTREAL and return.

A Reverse of Excursion No. 39.
RATE,   -   -   - $16.00

Excursion No. 41.

BOSTON to MONTREAL and return.

ROUTE GOING :

Boston to Nashua......... ....Boston & Maine R. R.
Nashua to Concord.......................Concord R. R.
Concord to Groveton, via Plymouth ..... Boston & Lowell R.R.(W.M.Div.)
Groveton to Montreal, via Richmond......Grand Trunk R'y.

ROUTE RETURNING :

Montreal to St. Johns...................Grand Trunk R'y.
St. Johns to White River Junction........Central Vermont R. R.
White River Junction to Concord.........Boston & Maine R. R.
Concord to Nashua.....................Concord R. R.
Nashua to Boston......................Boston & MaineR. R.

RATE,   -   -   - $16.00

Excursion No. 42.

BOSTON to MONTREAL and return.

A Reverse of Excursion No. 41.

RATE,   -   -   - $16.00

Excursion No. 43.

BOSTON to MONTREAL and return.

ROUTE GOING :

Boston to Fitchburg...................:......Fitchburg R. R.
Fitchburg to Bellows Falls..............Cheshire R. R.
Bellows Falls to St. Johns, via Rutland....Central Vermont R. R.
St. Johns to Montreal...................Grand Trunk R'y.

ROUTE RETURNING :

Montreal to Groveton, via Island Pond....Grand Trunk R'y.
Groveton to Concord, via Plymouth ......Boston & Lowell R.R.
Concord to Nashua.....................Concord R. R.
Nashua to Boston ....Boston & Maine R. R.

RATE,   -   - $16.00

Excursion No. 44.

BOSTON to MONTREAL and return.

A Reverse of Excursion No. 43.

RATE,   -   -   - $16.00

BOSTON to MONTREAL and return.

ROUTE GOING :

Boston to Portland.....................Rail or Steamer.
Portland to Montreal via Gorham.........Grand Trunk R'y.

ROUTE RETURNING :

Montreal to St. Johns ....Grand Trunk R'y.
St. Johns to White River Junction........Central Vermont R. R.
White River Junction to Concord.........Boston & Maine R. R.
Concord to Nashua ....Concord R. R.
Nashua to Boston......................Boston & Maine R. R.

RATE,   -   -   - $16.00

BOSTON to MONTREAL and return.

A Reverse of Excursion No. 45.

RATE,   -   -   - $16.00

BOSTON to MONTREAL and return.

ROUTE GOING :

Boston to Fitchburg....................Fitchburg R. R.
Fitchburg to Bellows Falls...............Cheshire R. R.
Bellows Falls to St. Johns via Rutland......Central Vermont R. R.
St. Johns to Montreal....................Grand Trunk R'y.

ROUTE RETURNING :

Montreal to Portland via Richmond.......Grand Trunk R'y.
Portland to Boston................. ....Rail or Steamer.

RATE,   -   -   - $16.00

BOSTON to MONTREAL and return.

A Reverse of Excursion No. 47.

RATE,   -   - $16.00

BOSTON to MONTREAL and return.

(LAKE MEMPHREMAGOG.)

ROUTE GOING :

Boston to Montreal........ .. ..Via White River Junc. or Rutland.

ROUTE RETURNING :

Montreal to Magog...................	Canadian Pacific R'y.
Magog to Newport.....................	Lake Memphremagog Steamer.
Newport to Wells River................	Boston & Maine R. R.
Wells River to Concord................	Boston & Lowell R.R. (W. M. Div.)
Concord to Nashua.....................	Concord R. R.
Nashua to Boston......................	Boston & Maine R. R.

RATE, - - - $17.25

Excursion No. 50.

BOSTON to MONTREAL and return.

A Reverse of Excursion No. 49.

RATE, - - - $17.25

Excursion No. 51.

BOSTON to MONTREAL and return.

ROUTE GOING :

Boston to Nashua......................	Boston & Maine R. R.
Nashua to Concord.....................	Concord R. R.
Concord to White River Junction........	Boston & Maine R. R.
White River Junction to St. Johns.......	Central Vermont R. R.
St. Johns to Montreal	Grand Trunk R'y.

ROUTE RETURNING :

Montreal to St. Johns	Grand Trunk R'y.
St. Johns to Burlington................	Central Vermont R. R.
Burlington to Fort Ticonderoga.........	Lake Champlain Steamers.
Fort Ticonderoga to Baldwin............	Del. & Hudson Canal Co's R. R
Baldwin to Caldwell....................	Lake George Steamers.
Caldwell to Rutland via Saratoga........	Del. & Hudson Canal Co's R. R.
Rutland to Bellows Falls................	Central Vermont R. R.
Bellows Falls to Fitchburg..............	Cheshire R. R.
Fitchburg to Boston....................	Fitchburg R. R.

RATE, - - - $21.45

Excursion No. 52.

BOSTON to MONTREAL and return.

A Reverse of Excursion No. 51.

RATE, - - - $21 45

Excursion No. 53.

BOSTON to MONTREAL (Rapids) and return.

ROUTE GOING :

Boston to Fitchburg............. ....Fitchburg R. R.
Fitchburg to Bellows Falls...............Cheshire R. R.
Bellows Falls to Rutland..,.............Central Vermont R. R.
Rutland to Caldwell via Saratoga.........Del. & Hudson Canal Co's R. R.
Caldwell to Baldwin...................Lake George Steamers.
Baldwin to Fort Ticonderoga ....Del. & Hudson Canal Co's R. R.
Fort Ticonderoga to Burlington ....Lake Champlain Steamers.
Burlington to Rouse's Point..............Central Vermont R. R.
Rouse's Point to Ogdensburg ....Ogdensburg & L. Champlain R. R.
Ogdensburg to Prescott...................Ferry.
Prescott to Montreal via Rapids..........Grand Trunk R'y or Steamer.

ROUTE RETURNING :

Montreal to St. Johns ....Grand Trunk R'y.
St. Johns to White River Junction... ... ...Central Vermont R. R.
White River Junction to Concord.........Boston & Maine R. R.
Concord to Nashua....................Concord R. R.
Nashua to Boston.......................Boston & Maine R. R.

RATE, - - - $26.25

Excursion No. 54.

BOSTON to MONTREAL and return.

ROUTE GOING :

Boston to Montreal......................Via White River Junc. or Rutland

ROUTE RETURNING :

Montreal to St. Johns ....Grand Trunk R'y.
St. Johns to Burlington............ ......Central Vermont R. R.
Burlington to Fort Ticonderoga ....Lake Champlain Steamers.
Fort Ticonderoga to Albany via Saratoga...Del. & Hudson Canal Co's R. R.
Albany to New York..................Hudson River Steamers.
New York to Boston ....Sound Lines Steamers.

RATE, - - - $21.60

Excursion No. 55.

BOSTON to MONTREAL and return.

A Reverse of Excursion No. 54.

RATE, - - $21.60

BOSTON to MONTREAL and return.

ROUTE GOING :

Boston to New York....................Sound Lines Steamers.
New York to Albany...................Hudson River Steamers.
Albany to Caldwell via Saratoga.........Del. & Hudson Canal Co's R. R.
Caldwell to Baldwin....................Lake George Steamers.
Baldwin to Fort Ticonderoga............Del. & Hudson Canal Co's R. R.
Fort Ticonderoga to Burlington..........Lake Champlain Steamers.
Burlington to St. Johns.................Central Vermont R. R.
St. Johns to Montreal ....Grand Trunk R'y.

ROUTE RETURNING :

Montreal to Boston.....................Via White River Junc. or Rutland.
       RATE,   -   -   - $23.60

BOSTON to MONTREAL and return.

A Reverse of Excursion No. 56.
       RATE,   -   -   - $23.60

BOSTON to OGDENSBURG and return.

ROUTE GOING :

Boston to Nashua. ....Boston & Maine R. R.
Nashua to Concord... ....Concord R. R.
Concord to White River Junction.........Boston & Lowell R. R.
White River Junction to Rouse's Point....Central Vermont R. R.
Rouse's Point to Ogdensburg............Central V't R.R. (O.& L.C. Div.)

ROUTE RETURNING :

Ogdensburg to Prescott..................Ferry.
Prescott to Montreal via Rapids..........Grand Trunk R'y or Steamer.
Montreal to Boston.....................Via White River Junc. or Rutland
       RATE,   -   -   - $20.00

BOSTON to OGDENSBURG and return.

ROUTE GOING :

Boston to Fitchburg ....Fitchburg R. R.
Fitchburg to Bellows Falls...............Cheshire R. R.
Bellows Falls to Rouse's Point via Rutland } Central Vermont R. R.
   and St. Albans.....................}
Rouse's Point to Ogdensburg............ Central Vermont R. R.

ROUTE RETURNING :

Ogdensburg to Prescott.................Ferry.
Prescott to Montreal via Rapids..........Grand Trunk R'y, or Steamer.
Montreal to Boston.....................Via White River Junc. or Rutland
       RATE,   -   -   - $20.00

Excursion No. 60.

BOSTON to ALEXANDRIA BAY and return.

Boston to Nashua......................Boston & Maine R. R.
Nashua to Concord.....................Concord R. R.
Concord to White River Junction.........Boston & Maine R. R.
White River Junction to Rouse's Point....Central Vermont R. R.
Rouse's Point to Ogdensburg............Central V't R.R. (O. & L. C. Div.)
Ogdensburg to Alexandria Bay...........Steamer.

Return same Route.

RATE,   -   -   - $18.50

Excursion No. 61.

BOSTON to OTTAWA and return.

Boston to Nashua ....Boston & Maine R. R.
Nashua to Concord.....................Concord R. R.
Concord to White River Junction..........Boston & Maine R. R.
White River Junction to Rouse's Point ....Central Vermont R. R.
Rouse's Point to Ottawa..................Canada Atlantic R'y.

Return same Route.

RATE,   -   -   - $18.00

Excursion No. 62.

BOSTON to OTTAWA and return.

Boston to Fitchburg......................Fitchburg R. R.
Fitchburg to Bellows Falls........   .....Cheshire R. R.
Bellows Falls to Rouse's Point via Rutland and St. Albans ....} Central Vermont R. R.
Rouse's Point to Ottawa..................Canada Atlantic R'y.

Return same Route.

RATE,   -   -   - $18.00

Excursion No. 63.

BOSTON to OTTAWA and return.

ROUTE GOING :

Boston to Nashua......................Boston & Maine R. R.
Nashua to Concord.....................Concord R. R.
Concord to White River Junction.........Boston & Maine R. R.
White River Junction to Rouse's Point.....Central Vermont R. R.
Rouse's Point to Ottawa................Canada Atlantic R'y.

ROUTE RETURNING:

Ottawa to Rouse's Point.................Canada Atlantic R'y.
Rouse's Point to Bellows Falls via Rutland..Central Vermont R. R.
Bellows Falls to Fitchburg...............Cheshire R. R.
Fitchburg to Boston.....................Fitchburg R. R.

RATE, - - - $18.00

Excursion No. 64.

BOSTON to OTTAWA and return.

Boston to Nashua ....Boston & Maine R. R.
Nashua to Concord.....................Concord R. R.
Concord to White River Junction........Boston & Maine R. R.
White River Junction to St. Johns.........Central Vermont R. R.
St. Johns to Coteau ....Grand Trunk R'y.
Coteau to Ottawa ....Canada Atlantic R. R.

Return same Route.

RATE, - - - $18.00

Excursion No. 65.

BOSTON to OTTAWA and return.

Boston to Fitchburg....................Fitchburg R. R.
Fitchburg to Bellows Falls..............Cheshire R. R.
Bellows Falls to St. Johns, via Rutland } Central Vermont R R
and Burlington................... }
St. Johns to Coteau.. ....Grand Trunk R'y.
Coteau to Ottawa ....Canada Atlantic R. R.

Return same Route.

RATE, - - - $18.00

Excursion No. 66.

BOSTON to OTTAWA and return.

ROUTE GOING:

Boston to Nashua ....Boston & Maine R. R.
Nashua to Concord.....................Concord R. R.
Concord to White River Junction..... ...Boston & Maine R. R.
White River Junction to St. Johns.......Central Vermont R. R.
St. Johns to Coteau....................Grand Trunk R'y.
Coteau to Ottawa......................Canada Atlantic R. R.

ROUTE RETURNING:

Ottawa to Lacolle. ....Canada Atlantic R. R.
Lacolle to Rouse's Point...............Grand Trunk Railway.
Rouse's Point to Bellows Falls, via Bur- } Central Vermont R. R.
lington and Rutland .... }
Bellows Falls to Fitchburg..............Cheshire R. R.
Fitchburg to Boston...................Fitchburg R. R.

RATE, - - - $18.00

QUEBEC was founded in 1608, by Samuel de Champlain on the site of the Indian village of Stadacona. No city on this Continent so impresses the traveler by the startling peculiarities of the site and novelty of its general aspect, as this Ancient Capital, or stamps its impress so indelibly on eye and memory. A massive wall of hewn stone, of nearly three miles in length, and varying, but everywhere of forbidding height and thickness, with projecting bastions and frowning cannon, encloses the better portion of the Upper Town, and has led to Quebec being called the "Great Walled City of the North." The citadel will, perhaps, prove the point of greatest interest to many, from the historical associations connected therewith, and from the fact that it is considered an impregnable

fortress. It covers an enclosed area of forty acres, and is some 340 feet above the river level. The zigzag passage through which you enter the fortress, between high and massive granite walls, is swept at every turn by formidable batteries of heavy guns. On the forbidding river walls and at each angle or possible commanding point, guns of heavy calibre sweep every avenue of approach by the river. Ditches, breastworks, and frowning batteries command the approaches by land, from the famed "Plains of Abraham." The precipitous bluffs, rising almost perpendicularly from the river 340 feet, present a natural barrier which may be swept with murderous fire, and the covered ways of approach and retreat, the various kinds and calibre of guns, mortars, howitzers and munitions of war, all awaken eager interest.

Among places of interest may be mentioned the Plains of Abraham ; the Governors' Garden, with its monument to Wolfe and Montcalm ; the spot where fell the American General Montgomery ; the City Gates ; the Roman Catholic Cathedral ; the Episcopal Cathedral ; the Houses of Parliament ; Laval University, etc., etc. The Falls of Montmorenci are situated in a beautiful nook of the river, about eight miles from Quebec. They are higher than those of Niagara, being more than 250 feet high, but are only some fifty feet wide. The drive to the falls is very beautiful ; the scenery on the road through Beauport, where the Provincial Lunatic Asylum is built, and back again is full of interest.

Excursion No. 67.

BOSTON to QUEBEC and return.

ROUTE GOING :

Boston to Nashua	Boston & Maine R. R.
Nashua to Concord	Concord R. R.
Concord to White River Junction	Boston & Maine R. R.
White River Junction to St. Johns	Central Vermont R. R.
St. Johns to Montreal	Grand Trunk R'y.
Montreal to Quebec	Rail or Steamer.

ROUTE RETURNING :

Quebec to Montreal	Rail or Steamer.
Montreal to Boston	Via White River Junc. or Rutland.

RATE, - - - $18 00

Excursion No. 68.

BOSTON to QUEBEC and return.

ROUTE GOING :

Boston to Fitchburg..............	Fitchburg R. R.
Fitchburg to Bellows Falls...............	Cheshire R. R.
Bellows Falls to St. Johns via Rutland and Burlington............	Central Vermont R. R.
St. Johns to Montreal...................	Grand Trunk R'y.
Montreal to Quebec	Rail or Steamer.

ROUTE RETURNING :

Quebec to Montreal....................	Rail or Steamer.
Montreal to Boston....................	Via White River Junc. or Rutland.

RATE,   -   -   - $18.00

Excursion No. 69.

BOSTON to QUEBEC and return.

ROUTE GOING :

Boston to Quebec	Via White River Junc. or Rutland and Montreal.

ROUTE RETURNING :

Quebec to Sherbrooke....................	Grand Trunk R'y.
Sherbrooke to Wells River...............	Boston & Maine R. R.
Wells River to Concord.................	Boston & Lowell R.R. (W. M. Div.)
Concord to Nashua....................	Concord R. R.
Nashua to Boston....................	Boston & Maine R. R.

RATE,   -   - $18.00

Excursion No. 70.

BOSTON to QUEBEC and return.

A Reverse of Excursion No. 69.

RATE, - - - $18.00

Excursion No. 71.

BOSTON to QUEBEC and return.

ROUTE GOING :
Boston to Quebec..................... { Via White River Junc. or Rutland and Montreal.

ROUTE RETURNING :
Quebec to Groveton.....................Grand Trunk R'y.
Groveton to Concord via Plymouth.......Boston & Lowell R.R. (W. M. Div.)
Concord to Nashua......................Concord R. R.
Nashua to Boston.......... ....Boston & Maine R. R.

RATE, - - - $18.00

Excursion No. 72

BOSTON to QUEBEC and return.

A Reverse of Excursion No. 71.

RATE, - - - $18.00

Excursion No. 73.

BOSTON to QUEBEC and return.

ROUTE GOING :
Boston to Quebec... .... { Via White River Junc. or Rutland and Montreal.

ROUTE RETURNING :
Quebec to Portland via Gorham.........Grand Trunk R'y.
Portland to Boston........ ....Rail or Steamer.

RATE, - - - $18.00

Excursion No. 74.

BOSTON to QUEBEC and return.

A Reverse of Excursion No. 73.

RATE, - - - $18.00

Excursion No. 75.

BOSTON to HA HA BAY and return.

(SAGUENAY RIVER.)

ROUTE GOING :

Boston to Quebec. { Via White River Junction, or Rutland and Montreal.

Quebec to Ha Ha Bay and return. . . . . Steamer.

ROUTE RETURNING :

Quebec to Boston . . . . Return by Selected Excursion.

RATE, - - - $26.00

Excursion No. 76.

BOSTON to QUEBEC via RAPIDS and return.

ROUTE GOING :

Boston to Ogdensburg. . . . . Via White River Junc. or Rutland.

Ogdensburg to Prescott. . . . . Ferry.

Prescott to Quebec via Rapids. . . . . Grand Trunk R'y or Steamer.

ROUTE RETURNING :

Quebec to Boston. . . . . Via Montreal or Sherbrooke.

RATE, - - - $23.50

Excursion No. 77.

BOSTON to QUEBEC and return.

ROUTE GOING :

Boston to Ottawa. . . . . : . . . { Via White River Junction, or Rutland and Rouse's Point.

Ottawa to Coteau. . . . . Canada Atlantic R'y.

Coteau to Montreal. . . . .Grand Trunk R'y.

Montreal to Quebec . . . . Rail or Steamer.

ROUTE RETURNING :

Quebec to Montreal. . . . . Rail or Steamer.

Montreal to Boston . . . . Via White River Junc. or Rutland.

RATE, - - - $23.00

PROVINCES

OF QUEBEC, NEW BRUNSWICK AND NOVA SCOTIA, WITH PRINCE EDWARD ISLAND.

—

Excursion No. 78.

BOSTON to ST. JOHN, N. B. and return.

ROUTE GOING :

Boston to Montreal........................Via White River Junc. or Rutland.
Montreal to Quebec.......................Rail or Steamer.
Quebec to Point Levi.....................Ferry.
Point Levi to St. John via Metapediac, } Intercolonial R'y.
   Miramichi and Moncton............ }

ROUTE RETURNING :

St. John to Boston via Portland.........International Steamship Co.

    RATE.   -   -   - $22.50

Excursion No. 79.

BOSTON to ST. JOHN, N. B. and return.

A Reverse of Excursion No. 78.

    RATE,   -   -   - $22.50

Excursion No. 80.

BOSTON to HALIFAX and return.

ROUTE GOING :

Boston to St. John via Portland.........International Steamship Co.
St. John to Halifax via Amherst.........Intercolonial R'y.

ROUTE RETURNING :

Halifax to Point Levi via Moncton, Mira- } Intercolonial R'y.
   michi and Metapediac.............. }
Point Levi to Quebec....................Ferry.
Quebec to Montreal......................Rail or Steamer.
Montreal to Boston......................Via White River Junc. or Rutland.

    RATE,   -   -   - $28.00

Excursion No. 81.

BOSTON to HALIFAX and return.

A Reverse of Excursion No. 80.

    RATE,   -   -   - $28.00

BOSTON to PRINCE EDWARD ISLAND and return.

ROUTE GOING :

Boston to Montreal......................Via White River Junc. or Rutland.
Montreal to Quebec......................Rail or Steamer.
Quebec to Point Levi....................Ferry.
Point Levi to Point du Chêne...........Intercolonial R'y.
Point du Chêne to Summerside ....Steamer.
Summerside to Charlottetown ....Price Edward Island R'y.

ROUTE RETURNING :

Charlottetown to Pictou.................Steamer.
Pictou to Halifax.......................Intercolonial R'y.
Halifax to St. John via Amherst.........International R'y.
St. John to Boston via Portland.........International Steamship Co.

RATE, - - - $34.00

Excursion No. 83.

BOSTON to PRINCE EDWARD ISLAND and return.

A Reverse of Excursion No. 82.

RATE, - - - $34.00

Excursions Nos. 79, 80 and 83 can be furnished *rail* from Boston, via Bangor to St. John, at $5.50 additional.

GULF OF ST. LAWRENCE AND MARITIME PROVINCES,

Via Black Diamond Steamship Company.

Elegant accommodations. All modern improvements. Meals and Stateroom berth included in fare. Tickets good to stop over. Steamer stops one day each at Charlottetown and Pictou, with two days' stop at St. Johns. Round-trip passengers can live on board while in port, without extra charge.

Excursion No. 84.

BOSTON to GULF OF ST. LAWRENCE and ST. JOHN, NEWFOUNDLAND.

Boston to Montreal......................Via White River Junc. or Rutland.
Thence by Black Diamond Steamship to follow points :

	one way	Return to Boston
Charlottetown, P. E. I.,	$29 50	$49 25
Pictou, N. S.,	30 00	50 00
St. Johns, N. F.,	38 00	66 00

BOSTON to GULF OF ST. LAWRENCE and HALIFAX.

ROUTE GOING :

Boston to Montreal .Via White River Junc. or Rutland.
Montreal to Pictou .Black Diamond Steamship Co.
Pictou to Halifax . . . . .Intercolonial R'y.

ROUTE RETURNING :

Halifax to St. John .Intercolonial R'y.
St. John to Boston .International Steamship Co.

RATE, - - - $41.25

BOSTON to ST. JOHN, NEWFOUNDLAND, and HALIFAX.

ROUTE GOING :

Boston to Montreal .Via White River Junc. or Rutland.
Montreal to St. Johns, N. F . . . . .Black Diamond Steamship Co.

ROUTE RETURNING :

St. Johns, N. F., to Pictou . . . . .Black Diamond Steamship Co.
Pictou to Halifax . . . . .Intercolonial R'y.
Halifax to St. John .Intercolonial R'y.
St. John to Boston .International Steamship Co.

RATE, - - - $59.25

The Adirondacks of New York have sprung into sudden and universal fame and favoritism. The region has all the novelty of a primeval land, diversified by every variety of landscape and unsearched solitudes ; and has the freshness and rare novelty of guides who alone know the secret wealth of this new paradise. The atmosphere is remarkably pure and free from malarious poisons and from chilling damps, so that sudden colds and tormenting fever heats are scarcely known. At present the Adirondacks may boast of its primeval charms ; but the region will, doubtless, be materially altered in this respect ere long, as visitors to this region are annually numbered by thousands.

In the valleys between the mountains lie many beautiful lakes and ponds, more than one thousand in number. The general level of these lakes is about 1500 feet above the sea, but Avalanche Lake, the highest of them, has nearly twice that elevation.

Some of them are twenty miles in length, while others cover only a few acres.

"Steep, densely-wooded mountains," says a writer in *Picturesque America*, describing these lakes, "rise from their margins; beautiful bays indent their borders, and leafy points jut out; spring brooks trickle in, while the shallows are fringed with water-grasses and flowering plants, and covered sometimes with acres of white and yellow water-lilies. The lakes are all lovely and romantic in everything except their names; and the scenery they offer in combination with the towering mountains and the old and savage forests, is not surpassed on earth. In natural features it greatly resembles Switzerland and the Scottish Highlands as they must have been before those regions were settled and cultivated." This labyrinth of lakes is connected by a very intricate system of rivers, rivulets and brooks.

The following Excursions can be furnished either via Lowell, Concord, and White River Junction, or via Fitchburg, Bellows Falls and Rutland. Also to go one route and return the other, between Boston and the stage or steamer point.

If desired different from the route given, mention must be made of desired route at time of purchase.

Excursion No. 87.

BOSTON to RALPHS (Upper Chateaugay Lake) and return.

Boston to Nashua	Boston & Maine R. R.
Nashua to Concord	Concord R. R.
Concord to White River Junction	Boston & Maine R. R.
White River Junction to Rouse's Point	Central Vermont R. R.
Rouse's Point to Chateaugay	Central V't R.R. (O. & L. C. Div.)
Chateaugay to Lower Chateaugay Lake	Stage, 6 miles.
Lower Chateaugay Lake to Ralphs	Steamer.

Return same Route.

RATE, - - - $16.50

Excursion No. 88.

BOSTON to LOON LAKE and return.

Boston to Nashua	Boston & Maine R. R.
Nashua to Concord	Concord R. R.
Concord to White River Junction	Boston & Maine R. R.
White River Junction to Rouse's Point	Central Vermont R. R.
Rouse's Point to Malone	Central V't R.R. (O. & L. C. Div)
Malone to Loon Lake House	Stage, 29 miles.

Return same Route.

RATE. - - - $17.75

BOSTON to MEACHAM LAKE and return.

Boston to Nashua......................Boston & Maine R. R.
Nashua to Concord............ ....Concord R. R.
Concord to White River Junction........Boston & Maine R. R.
White River Junction to Rouse's Point....Central Vermont R. R.
Rouse's Point to Malone.................Central V't R.R. (O. & L. C. Div.)
Malone to Meacham Lake House........Stage, 25 miles.
Return same Route.
RATE, - - - $21.00

BOSTON to BLUE MOUNTAIN HOUSE and return.

Boston to Nashua......................Boston & Maine R. R.
Nashua to Concord.......................Concord R. R.
Concord to White River Junction........Boston & Maine R. R.
White River Junction to Rouse's Point...Central Vermont R. R.
Rouse's Point to Moira.................Central V't R.R. (O. & L. C. Div.)
Moira to Spring Cove...................Northern Adirondack R. R.
Spring Cove to Blue Mountain House....Stage, 4 miles.
Return same Route.
RATE, - - - $18.70

BOSTON to PAUL SMITH'S and return.

Boston to Nashua......................Boston & Maine R. R.
Nashua to Concord ....Concord R. R.
Concord to White River Junction........Boston & Maine R. R.
White River Junction to Rouse's Point...Central Vermont R. R.
Rouse's Point to Moira.................Central V't R.R. (O. & L. C. Div.)
Moira to Paul Smith's Station...........Northern Adirondack R. R.
Paul Smith's Station to Paul Smith's.....Stage, 7 miles.
Return same Route.
RATE, - - - $19.90

BOSTON to PAUL SMITH'S and return.

Boston to Fitchburg....................Fitchburg R. R.
Fitchburg to Bellows Falls..............Cheshire R. R.
Bellows Falls to Rouse's Point..........Central Vermont R. R.
Rouse's Point to Moira.................Central V't R.R. (O. & L. C. Div.)
Moira to Paul Smith's Station ....Northern Adirondack R. R.
Paul Smith's Station to Paul Smith's.....Stage, 7 miles.
Return same Route.
RATE, - - $19.50

Excursion No. 90 B.

BOSTON to LAKE PLACID and return.

ROUTE GOING :

Boston to Nashua.........................Boston & Maine R. R.
Nashua to Concord.......................Concord R. R.
Concord to White River Junction..........Boston & Maine R. R.
White River Junction to Burlington.......Central Vermont R. R.
Burlington to Plattsburgh................Steamer.
Plattsburgh to Loon Lake Station.........Chateaugay R. R.
Loon Lake Station to Lake Placid.........Stage.

ROUTE RETURNING :

Lake Placid to Paul Smith's..............Stage.
Paul Smith's to Paul Smith's Station.....Stage.
Paul Smith's Station to Moira............No. Adirondack R. R.
Moira to White River Junction............Central Vermont R. R.
White River Junction to Concord ....Boston & Maine R. R.
Concord to Nashua ....Concord R. R.
Nashua to Boston.........................Boston & Maine R. R.
RATE, - - - $23.70

Excursion No. 90 C.

BOSTON to LAKE PLACID and return.

ROUTE GOING :

Boston to Fitchburg......................Fitchburg R. R.
Fitchburg to Bellows Falls...............Cheshire R. R.
Bellows Falls to Rutland ....Central Vermont R. R.
Rutland to Westport via Saratoga.........Del. & Hudson Canal Co's R. R.
Westport to Lake Placid via Elizabethtown..Stage.

ROUTE RETURNING :

Lake Placid to Paul Smith's..............Stage.
Paul Smith's to Paul Smith's Station.....Stage.
Paul Smith's Station to Moira............No. Adirondack R. R.
Moira to Bellows Falls...................Central Vermont R. R.
Bellows Falls to Fitchburg ....Cheshire R. R.
Fitchburg to Boston......................Fitchburg R. R.
RATE, $23.70

Excursion No. 90 D.

BOSTON to LAKE PLACID and return.

ROUTE GOING :

Boston to Fitchburg......................Fitchburg R. R.
Fitchburg to Bellows Falls...............Cheshire R.R.
Bellows Falls to Rutland ....Central Vermont R. R.
Rutland to Westport via Saratoga.........Del. & Hudson Canal Co's R. R.
Westport to Lake Placid..................Stage.

ROUTE RETURNING :

Lake Placid to Loon Lake Station.........Stage.
Loon Lake Station to Plattsburgh.........Chateaugay R. R.
Plattsburgh to Burlington................Steamer.
Burlington to White River Junction.......Central Vermont R. R.
White River Junction to Concord ....Boston & Maine R. R.
Concord to Nashua........................Concord R. R.
Nashua to Boston.........................Boston & Maine R. R.
RATE, - - - - - $23.70

Excursion No. 90 E.

BOSTON to SARANAC INN (Prospect House) and return.

Boston to Nashua........................Boston & Maine R. R.
Nashua to Concord......................Concord R. R.
Concord to White River Junction.......Boston & Maine R. R.
White River Junction to Rouse's Point...Central Vermont R. R.
Rouse's Point to Moira.................Central V't R.R. (O. & L. C. Div.)
Moira to Paul Smith's Station..........Northern Adirondack R. R.
Paul Smith's Station to Prospect House...Stage, 15 miles.

Return same Route.

RATE, - - - $21.20

Excursion No. 90 F.

BOSTON to SARANAC LAKE HOUSE and return.

Boston to Fitchburg....................Fitchburg R. R.
Fitchburg to Bellows Falls.............Cheshire R. R.
Bellows Falls to Rouse's Point.........Central Vermont R. R.
Rouse's Point to Moira.................Central V't R.R. (O. & L. C. Div.)
Moira to Paul Smith's Station..........Northern Adirondack R.R.
Paul Smith's Sta'n to Saranac Lake House.Stage, 17 miles.

Return same Route.

RATE, - - - $21.00

Excursion No. 91.

BOSTON to LYON MOUNTAIN and return.

Boston to Fitchburg....................Fitchburg R. R.
Fitchburg to Bellows Falls.............Cheshire R. R.
Bellows Falls to Burlington via Rutland...Central Vermont R. R.
Burlington to Plattsburg...............Steamer.
Plattsburg to Lyon Mountain............Chateaugay R. R.

Return same Route.

RATE, - - - $17.30

Excursion No. 92.

BOSTON to SARANAC LAKE and return.

Boston to Fitchburg....................Fitchburg R. R.
Fitchburg to Bellows Falls.............Cheshire R. R.
Bellows Falls to Burlington via Rutland....Central Vermont R. R.
Burlington to Plattsburgh..............Steamer.
Plattsburg to Saranac Lake.............Chateaugay R. R.

Return same Route.

RATE, - - $18.50

BOSTON to PAUL SMITH'S and return.

Boston to Fitchburg....................Fitchburg R. R.
Fitchburg to Bellows Falls..............Cheshire R. R.
Bellows Falls to Burlington via Rutland....Central Vermont R. R.
Burlington to Plattsburg................Steamer.
Plattsburg to Bloomingdale..............Chateaugay R. R.
Bloomingdale to Paul Smith's...........Stage.

Return same Route.

RATE,   -   -   - $19.90

BOSTON to ALEXANDRIA BAY and return.

ROUTE GOING :

Boston to Fitchburg................. ..Fitchburg R. R.
Fitchburg to Bellows Falls..............Cheshire R. R.
Bellows Falls to Rutland ....Central Vermont R. R.
Rutland to Schenectady.................Del. & Hudson Canal Co's R. R.
Schenectady to Utica............, ...N. Y. Cent. & Hudson River R. R.
Utica to Clayton via Trenton Falls......Utica & Black River R. R.
Clayton to Alexandria Bay..............Steamer.

ROUTE RETURNING :

Alexandria Bay to Ogdensburg..........Steamer.
Ogdensburg to Rouse's Point............Central V't R.R. (O. & L C. Div.)
Rouse's Point to White River Junction....Central Vermont R. R.
White River Junction to Concord........Boston & Maine R. R.
Concord to Nashua.....................Concord R. R.
Nashua to Boston.....................Boston & Maine R. R.

RATE,   -   -   - $19.00

BOSTON to ALEXANDRIA BAY and return.

ROUTE GOING :

Boston to Alexandria Bay..............Excursion No. 94.

ROUTE RETURNING :

Alexandria Bay to Montreal via Rapids...Steamer.
Montreal to Boston.....................Via White River Junc. or Rutland.

RATE, $22.65

Excursion No. 96.

BOSTON to ALEXANDRIA BAY and return.

ROUTE GOING :

Boston to New York....................Sound Line Steamers.
New York to Albany....................Hudson River Steamers.
Albany to Utica.........................N. Y. Cent. & Hudson River R. R.
Utica to Clayton.......................Utica & Black River R. R.
Clayton to Alexandria Bay.............Steamer.

ROUTE RETURNING :

Alexandria Bay to Boston..............Excursion No. 94.

RATE, - - - $21.80

Excursion No. 97.

BOSTON to ALEXANDRIA BAY and return

ROUTE GOING :

Boston to Alexandria Bay..............Excursion No. 96.

ROUTE RETURNING :

Alexandria Bay to Montreal via Rapids...Steamer.
Montreal to Boston....................Via White River Junc. or Rutland.

RATE, - - - $24.65

THE WHITE MOUNTAINS.

" Thou who wouldst see the lovely and the wild
Mingled in harmony on Nature's face,
Ascend our rocky mountains. Let thy foot
Fail not with weariness, for on their tops
The beauty and the majesty of earth
Spread wide beneath, shall make thee to forget
The steep and toilsome way. There, as thou stand'st,
The haunts of men below thee, and around
The mountain summits, thy expanding heart
Shall feel a kindred with that loftier world
To which thou art translated, and partake
The enlargement of thy vision. Thou shalt look
Upon the green and rolling forest tops
And down into the secrets of the glens,
And streams, that with their bordering thickets strive
To hide their windings. Thou sha't gaze, at once,
Here on white villages, and tilth and herds,
And swarming roads, and there on solitudes,
That only hear the torrent, and the wind,
And eagle's shriek.

. . . .

To stand upon the beetling verge, and see
Where storm and lightning, from that huge gray wall,
Have tumbled down vast blocks, and at the base
Dashed them in fragments, and to lay thine ear
Over the dizzy depth, and hear the sound
Of winds that struggle with the woods below,
Come up like ocean murmurs. But the scene
Is lovely round."—*Bryant.*

THE PLUME, WHITE MOUNTAINS.

Excursion No, 98.

BOSTON to PROFILE HOUSE and return.

(WHITE MOUNTAINS.)

ROUTE GOING :

Boston to Nashua	Boston & Maine R. R.
Nashua to Concord	Concord R. R.
Concord to Plymouth	Boston & Lowell R.R. (W. M. Div.)
Plymouth to North Woodstock	Pemigewasset Valley R. R.
North Woodstock to Profile House	Stage.

ROUTE RETURNING:

Profile House to Bethlehem Junction..... Profile and Franconia Notch R. R.
Bethlehem Junction to Wells River ...... Boston & Lowell R.R. (W. M. Div.)
Wells River to White River Junction...... Boston & Maine R. R.
White River Junction to Windsor.......... Central Vermont R. R.
Windsor to Bellows Falls . ... Vermont Valley R. R.
Bellows Falls to Fitchburg .... Cheshire R. R.
Fitchburg to Boston .... Fitchburg R. R.

RATE,   - - - $13.45

Excursion No. 99.

BOSTON to PROFILE HOUSE and return.

A Reverse of Excursion No. 98.

RATE,   - - - $13.45

Excursion No. 100.

BOSTON to CRAWFORD HOUSE and return.

ROUTE GOING:

Boston to Nashua .... Boston & Maine R. R.
Nashua to Concord..................... Concord R. R.
Concord to Plymouth .... Boston & Maine R. R.
Plymouth to North Woodstock .... Pemigewasset Valley R. R.
North Woodstock to Profile House........ Stage.
Profile House to Bethlehem Junction...... Profile and Franconia Notch R. R
Bethlehem Junction to Fabyan's.......... Boston & Lowell R.R. (W. M. Div.)
Fabyan's to Crawford .... Maine Central R. R.

ROUTE RETURNING:

Crawford to Fabyan's .... Maine Central R. R.
Fabyan's to Wells River................. Boston & Lowell R.R. (W. M Div.)
Wells River to White River Junction...... Passumpsic R. R.
White River Junction to Windsor........ Central Vermont R. R.
Windsor to Bellows Falls................ Vermont Valley R. R.
Bellows Falls to Fitchburg.............. Cheshire R. R.
Fitchburg to Boston .... Fitchburg R. R.

RATE,   - - - $14.75

Excursion No. 101.

BOSTON to CRAWFORD HOUSE and return.

A Reverse of Excursion No. 100.

RATE,   - - - $14.75

7

Excursion No. 102.

BOSTON to FABYAN'S and return.

ROUTE GOING :

Boston to Fitchburg..................Fitchburg R. R.
Fitchburg to Bellows Falls ....Cheshire R. R.
Bellows Falls to Windsor ....Vermont Valley R. R.
Windsor to White River Junction.........Central Vermont R. R.
White River Junction to Wells River......Boston & Maine R. R.
Wells River to Bethlehem Junction ....Boston & Lowell R.R. (W. M. Div.)
Bethlehem Junc. to Fabyan's ....Boston & Lowell R.R. (W. M. Div.)

ROUTE RETURNING :

Fabyan's to No. Conway via Notch.......Maine Central R. R.
North Conway to Wolfboro.............Boston & Maine R. R.
Wolfboro to Weirs via Centre Harbor ....Lake Winnipesaukee Steamers
Weirs to Concord ....Boston & Lowell R.R. (W. M. Div.)
Concord to Nashua ....Concord R. R.
Nashua to Boston ....Boston & Maine R. R.

RATE,   •   •   • $14.80

Excursion No. 103.

BOSTON to FABYAN'S and return.

A Reverse of Excursion No. 102.

RATE, $14.80

Excursion No. 104.

BOSTON to FABYAN'S and return.

ROUTE GOING :

Boston to Fabyan's................... { Choice of Routes via Portland, North Conway or Concord.

ROUTE RETURNING :

Fabyan's to Wells River.................Boston & Lowell R.R. (W. M. Div.)
Wells River to White River Junction......Boston & Maine R. R.
White River Junction to Windsor.........Central Vermont R. R.
Windsor to Bellows Falls.................Vermont Valley R. R.
Bellows Falls to Fitchburg ....Cheshire R. R.
Fitchburg to Boston ....Fitchburg R. R.

RATE,   -   - .   - $12.00

BOSTON to FABYAN'S and return.

ROUTE GOING :

Boston to Fitchburg ....Fitchburg R. R.
Fitchburg to Bellows Falls ....Cheshire R. R.
Bellows Falls to Windsor ....Vermont Valley R. R.
Windsor to White River Junction...... .Central Vermont R. R.
White River Junction to Wells River ....Boston & Maine R. R.
Wells River to Fabyan's................Boston & Lowell R.R. (W. M. Div.)

"OLD MAN OF THE MOUNTAINS."

ROUTE RETURNING :

Fabyan's to Boston.................... { Choice of Routes via Portland, North Conway or Concord.

RATE,   -   -   -   **$12.00**

Excursion No. 106.

BOSTON to MOUNT WASHINGTON and return.

ROUTE GOING :

Boston to Portland.....................Rail or Steamer.
Portland to Gorham ....Grand Trunk R'y.
Gorham to Glen House...................Stage.
Glen House to Summit Mount Washington and return................. } Carriages.

ROUTE RETURNING :

Glen House to Glen Station via Crystal Cascade, Glen Ellis Falls and Pinkham Notch........................ } Stage.
Glen Station to Fabyan's.................Maine Central R. R.
Fabyan's to Wells River via Twin M. House and Bethlehem Junction...... } Boston & Lowell R.R. (W. M. Div.)
Wells River to White River Junction......Boston & Maine R. R.
White River Junction to Windsor.........Central Vermont R. R.
Windsor to Bellows Falls................Vermont Valley R. R.
Bellows Falls to Fitchburg..............Cheshire R. R.
Fitchburg to Boston.....................Fitchburg R. R.

RATE,   -   -   -   **$22.00**

Excursion No. 107.

BOSTON to MOUNT WASHINGTON and return.

A Reverse of Excursion No. 1c6.

RATE,   -   -   -   **$22.00**

Excursion No. 108.

BOSTON to MONTREAL and return.

ROUTE GOING :

Boston to Nashua.......................Boston & Maine R. R.
Nashua to Concord.....................Concord R. R.
Concord to White River Junction.........Boston & Maine R. R.
White River Junction to St. Johns........Central Vermont R. R.
St. Johns to Montreal...................Grand Trunk R'y.

ROUTE RETURNING :

Montreal to St. Johns...................Grand Trunk R'y.
St. Johns to Montpelier.................Central Vermont R. R.
Montpelier to Wells River..............Montpelier & Wells River R. R.
Wells River to Fabyan's................Boston & Lowell R.R. (W. M. Div.)
Fabyan's to Boston.................. { Choice of Routes via Portland, No. Conway or Concord.

RATE,   -   -   -   **$18.50**

Excursion No. 109.

BOSTON to QUEBEC and return.

ROUTE GOING :

Boston to Fabyan's.....................	{ Choice of Routes via Portland, No. Conway or Concord.
Fabyan's to Lunenburg............... ...Boston & Lowell R.R. (W. M. Div.)
Lunenburg to St. Johnsbury............St. Johnsbury & I. Champlain R.R.
St. Johnsbury to Sherbrooke............Boston & Maine R. R.
Sherbrooke to Point Levi...............Grand Trunk R'y.
Point Levi to Quebec...................Ferry

ROUTE RETURNING :

Quebec to Montreal...... ....Rail or Steamer.
Montreal to Boston ....Via White River Junc. or **Rutland.**

RATE, - - - $21.45

Excursion No. 110.

BOSTON to QUEBEC and return.

A Reverse of Excursion No. 109.

RATE, - - - $21.45

Excursion No. 111.

BOSTON to BURLINGTON and return.

ROUTE GOING :

Boston to Fabyan's.....................	{ Choice of Routes via Portland, North Conway or Concord.
Fabyan's to Wells River............. ...Boston & Lowell R.R. (W. M. Div.)
Wells River to Montpelier...............Montpelier & Wells River R. R.
Montpelier to Burlington ....Central Vermont R. R.

ROUTE RETURNING :

Burlington to Fort Ticonderoga...........Lake Champlain Steamers.
Fort Ticonderoga to Rutland via Saratoga. Del. & Hudson Canal Co's R. R.
Rutland to Bellows Falls ....Central Vermont R. R.
Bellows Falls to Fitchburg...............Cheshire R. R.
Fitchburg to Boston ....Fitchburg R. R.

RATE, - - - $19.60

Excursion No. 112.

BOSTON to BURLINGTON and return.

A Reverse of Excursion No. 111.

RATE, - - - $19.60

Excursion No. 113.

BOSTON to LAKE GEORGE and return.

ROUTE GOING :

Boston to Fitchburg	Fitchburg R. R.
Fitchburg to Bellows Falls	Cheshire R. R.
Bellows Falls to Rutland	Central Vermont R. R.
Rutland to Caldwell via Saratoga	Del. & Hudson Canal Co's R. R.

ROUTE RETURNING :

Caldwell to Baldwin	Lake George Steamers.
Baldwin to Fort Ticonderoga	Del. & Hudson Canal Co's R. R.
Fort Ticonderoga to Burlington	Lake Champlain Steamers.
Burlington to Montpelier	Central Vermont R. R.
Montpelier to Wells River	Montpelier & Wells River R. R.
Wells River to Fabyan's	Boston & Lowell R. R.
Fabyan's to Boston	Choice of Routes via Portland, North Conway or Concord.

RATE, - - - $21.90

Excursion No. 114.

BOSTON to LAKE GEORGE and return.

A Reverse of Excursion No. 113.

RATE, - - - $21.90

Excursion No. 115.

BOSTON to LAKE CHAMPLAIN and return.

ROUTE GOING :

Boston to New York	Sound Lines Steamers.
New York to Albany	Hudson River Steamers.
Albany to Fort Ticonderoga via Saratoga	Del. & Hudson Canal Co's R. R.
Fort Ticonderoga to Burlington	Lake Champlain Steamers.

ROUTE RETURNING :

Burlington to Montpelier	Central Vermont R. R.
Montpelier to Wells River	Montpelier & Wells River R. R.
Wells River to Fabyan's	Boston & Lowell R. R.
Fabyan's to Boston	Choice of Routes via Portland, North Conway or Concord.

RATE, - - - $21.60

Excursion No. 116.

BOSTON to LAKE CHAMPLAIN and return.

A Reverse of Excursion No. 115.

RATE, - - - $21.60

Excursion No. 117.

BOSTON to LAKE GEORGE and return.

ROUTE GOING :

Boston to Fabyan's.....................	{ Choice of Routes via Portland, North Conway or Concord.
Fabyan's to Wells River......'..........	Boston & Lowell R. R.
Wells River to Montpelier...............	Montpelier & Wells River R. R.
Montpelier to Burlington.................	Central Vermont R. R.
Burlington to Fort Ticonderoga...........	Lake Champlain Steamers.
Fort Ticonderoga to Baldwin.............	Del. & Hudson Canal Co's R. R.
Baldwin to Caldwell.....................	Lake George Steamers.

ROUTE RETURNING :

Caldwell to Albany via Saratoga..........	Del. & Hudson Canal Co's R. R.
Albany to New York.....................	Hudson River Steamers.
New York to Boston.....................	Sound Lines Steamers.

RATE, - - - $23.40

Excursion No. 118.

BOSTON to LAKE GEORGE and return.

A Reverse of Excursion No. 117.

RATE, - - - $23.40

NIAGARA FALLS.—"We stand in view of one of the grandest scenes on earth! Our vocabularies are hastily ransacked for their biggest and most enthusiastic adjectives to characterize the magnificent sublimity, wild majesty and terrific grandeur of the scene!

"The mighty river of blue-green waters surging and dashing and tossing its white arms of foam, amid the mad rapids, then shuddering on the brink of the awful precipice, and plunging headlong into the yawning chasm below; the whirling and swirling of the floods; the thunderous roar that shakes the solid earth; the vast sheets of spray and mist, and the sunbeams that, caught in their liquid meshes, die like aerial dolphins in a blaze of a many-tinted pain; the rainbow that casts its resplendent arch across the majestic canyon; the glorious Horseshoe, the American Falls and all the lesser divisions of creation's greatest cataract; the tiny green islands that look as if any moment might see them swept down into the dizzy depths; an ocean pouring over rocky battlements into a bottomless abyss of waters; and through and over it all the everlasting thunder of the falling flood.

"Who, that has ever seen and heard all this commingled grandeur, beauty, sublimity and awfulness, can forget it while life and memory last? It is one of the wonders of the world; and, from the day that Father Hennepin and the hardy warriors of La Salle stood awestruck and dumb before it two hundred years ago, earth's greatest scholars, poets, orators and artists have striven in vain, with tongue and pen and pencil, to depict the veriest atom of its majesty and its glory. The little Frenchman came as near doing justice to it as far more pretentious enthusiasts have ever done, when, standing amid its spray and rainbows and eternal roar, he clapped his hands in rapture and exclaimed: 'Supairb! Magnifique! By gar, don't he come down bully!'"

The Thousand Islands are identified with many incidents of the earliest history of our country, and though it is only recently its peculiar beauty and fitness as a resting-place "amid the toil of the years" has become generally known to the people, yet, from east, west, north and south, its praises are sounded by those who have been made glad by its beauty. The air is light, dry and mellow, and is adapted to the constitution of almost every one. Fogs rarely occur here, neither is the night atmosphere damp.

The Indians in their rude, but poetic natures, called this locality "Manatoana," or Garden of the Great Spirit, and the name would seem to have been a most appropriate one, as applied to the spot when Nature ruled alone; when every island was a miniature forest;

when the wild deer made their homes in the island depths, and swam from point to point, and each secluded bay, nestling among the hills and bluffs, teemed with fowl that were never disturbed by harsh words, it was emphatically a garden in the wilderness. Even at this day there are hundreds of places, wild and solitary as in the primeval days; little watery nooks where the health-imparting resinous odors of the evergreens fill the gratified nostrils, and the whispers of Nature's mystic life serve but to make the solitude more blissful.

"As the steamer glides out into the delicious coolness and cleanliness of the open river, through scenery suggestive at every turn of exquisite beauty and romance, if you do not say, as was said of the wise king of old, 'The half has not been told,' then indeed it will be hard to meet with your approval. Soon your steamer passes in among the islands, and the bright sunlight falls upon the clear, pale, emerald waters, which in turn reflects back the islets it bears upon its surface, revealing successively their vales, glens or heights in all their sylvan or rugged beauty. At times our steamer passes so close to these islands that a pebble may be cast upon their shores, while, looking ahead, it appears as though further progress was barred, but rounding the points amid winding passages and bays the way is gradually opened before us. Again the river seems to come to an abrupt termination. Approaching the threatening shores a channel suddenly appears, and you are whirled into a magnificent amphitheatre of lake, that is, to all appearance, bounded by an immense green bank. As you draw near the mass is moved, as if in a kaleidoscope, and a hundred little isles appear in its place."

Having passed through the Lake of the Thousand Islands, we enter the River St. Lawrence. The increasing swiftness of the current reveals the fact that we are approaching one of those remarkable and celebrated

Rapids of the St. Lawrence.—The experience of shooting the rapids has been thus described :

"The increasing speed, and especially the perceptible descent, soon awaken the interest of the dullest among the passengers, and as the boat lurches to the right or left (or, in nautical phrase, to the starboard or port), to escape destruction from some ledge which the trusty pilot knows how to avoid, the excitement deepens and increases, and the half hour required for the passage of the Long Sault is crowded full of alternating delight, fear and exhilaration, quickening the pulse and giving zest to the journey, not to be appreciated except by those who experience it. At the foot of this rapid the placid waters of Lake St. Francis are entered, and the contrast between the tranquil surroundings and the tumult and excitement just passed through brings a grateful sense of relief, and the lovely scenery among which the boat now glides for twenty-five miles is all the more keenly appreciated. Passing Coteau du Lac, we enter the Coteau Rapids, descending quickly to the Cedars, Split Rock and Cascade Rapids. In passing the Cedars a peculiar sensation is experienced, as the boat appears to settle down occasionally with great suddenness, as though about to be submerged. This is supposed to be owing to a strong undercurrent which exerts this influence on the boat as she passes from one ledge of rock to another, although they are at a safe distance below her keel. The passage of the Split Rock Rapids seems dangerous, as indeed it would be were the pilot to forget for a moment the grave responsibility of his trust, and fail to swerve the boat at just the right moment to avoid some sharp rock or ledge that threatens destruction to the craft.

"The Cascades are so called from their resemblance to a series of short, leaping falls. Passing the Cascades we enter upon another broad expanse of water, the river here widening into Lake St. Louis, receiving also the waters of the Ottawa River. This lake is twelve miles long by about six in breadth, and the ride across its quiet waters just precedes the culminating excitement of the trip—the daring passage of the FAMOUS LACHINE RAPIDS.

"At the head of these Rapids is the pretty little village of Lachine, and here comes on board our Indian pilot, Baptiste by name, who has piloted the boats through the Lachine Rapids for forty years.

These rapids are the most perilous in all the river's extent on account of the devious nature of the channel, and the dangerous rocks which lie just enough below the surface to deceive any but the skillful navigator. The swarthy giant who takes the wheel at this point pays little attention to anything but the duty in hand, and that seems to demand all his energies. Casting alternate glances at him and at the rushing waters ahead of us, we involuntarily breathe the words of the hymn,

'Steady, O pilot, stand firm at the wheel.'

"Right in our path lies a ragged rock, which threatens us with instant destruction; but a turn of the wheel at just the right moment sends our good craft a little to the left of it, and the apparent danger is past. With bated breath we watch for the next peril that looms ahead of us, to find it, like its predecessor, vanquished by the strong arm and steady nerve of the man to whom every inch of the channel is as familiar as a beaten path.

"Entering once more into quiet waters we steam on our way toward Montreal, and soon the horizon is marked with the long line of the famous VICTORIA BRIDGE, which rises higher and higher as we approach it, until we glide under it and are soon at the wharf."

Excursions Nos. 119 to 131, inclusive, can be furnished via Sound Lines to New York, Hudson River Day Line to Albany; thence rail, at $1.50 additional.

Excursion No. 119.

BOSTON to NIAGARA FALLS and return.

ROUTE GOING:

Boston to Niagara Falls.............. { Choice of Routes via Rutland, Troy or Albany.

ROUTE RETURNING:

Niagara Falls to Montreal .... { Choice of Routes via Thousand Islands and Rapids, or all rail.
Montreal to St. Johns ....Grand Trunk R'y.
St. Johns to White River Junction..........Central Vermont R. R.
White River Junction to Concord ....'....Boston & Maine R. R.
Concord to Nashua......................Concord R. R.
Nashua to Boston ....Boston & Maine R. R.

RATE,   -   -   - $30.00

Excursion No. 120.

BOSTON to NIAGARA FALLS and return.

ROUTE GOING:

Montreal to Niagara Falls............. { Choice of Routes via Rutland, Troy or Albany.

ROUTE RETURNING:

Niagara Falls to Montreal............. { Choice of Routes via Thousand Islands and Rapids, or all rail.
Montreal to St. Johns ....Grand Trunk R'y.
St. Johns to Bellows Falls via Burlington } Central Vermont R. R
  and Rutland......................
Bellows Falls to Fitchburg...............Cheshire R. R.
Fitchburg to Boston ....Fitchburg R. R.

RATE,   -   - $30.00

Excursion No. 121.

BOSTON to NIAGARA FALLS and return.

ROUTE GOING :

Boston to Niagara Falls .... Choice of Routes via Rutland, Troy or Albany.

ROUTE RETURNING :

Niagara Falls to Ogdensburg........... Choice of Routes via Thousand Is. lands and Rapids, or all rail.

Ogdensburg to Rouse's Point ....Central V't R.R. (O. & L. C. Div.)
Rouse's Point to White River Junction....Central Vermont R. R.
White River Junction to Concord.........Boston & Maine R. R.
Concord to Nashua......................Concord R. R.
Nashua to Boston.......................Boston & Maine R. R.

RATE, - - - $30.00

Excursion No. 122.

BOSTON to NIAGARA FALLS and return.

ROUTE GOING :

Boston to Niagara Falls............... Choice of Routes via Rutland, Troy or Albany.

ROUTE RETURNING :

Niagara Falls to Ogdensburg........... Choice of Routes via Thousand Is. lands and Rapids, or all rail.

Ogdensburg to Rouse's Point............Central V't R.R. (O. & L. C. Div.)
Rouse's Point to Bellows Falls via Burlington and Rutland............... Central Vermont R. R.
Bellows Falls to Fitchburg ....Cheshire R. R.
Fitchburg to Boston....................Fitchburg R. R.

RATE, - - - $30.00

Excursion No. 123.

BOSTON to NIAGARA FALLS and return.

ROUTE GOING :

Boston to Niagara Falls............... Choice of Routes via Rutland, Troy or Albany.

ROUTE RETURNING :

Niagara Falls to Montreal..... .... Choice of Routes via Thousand Islands and Rapids, or all rail.

Montreal to St. Johns ....Grand Trunk R'y.
St. Johns to Burlington................Central Vermont R. R.
Burlington to Fort Ticonderoga ....Lake Champlain Steamers.
Fort Ticonderoga to Baldwin............Del. & Hudson Canal Co's R. R.
Baldwin to Caldwell................ .....Lake George Steamers.
Caldwell to Rutland, via Saratoga........Del. & Hudson Canal Co's R. R.
Rutland to Bellows Falls................Central Vermont R. R.
Bellows Falls to Fitchburg..............Cheshire R. R.
Fitchburg to Boston....................Fitchburg R. R.

RATE, - - $35.60

Excursion No. 124.

BOSTON to NIAGARA FALLS and return.

ROUTE GOING :

Boston to Niagara Falls................ { Choice of Routes via Rutland, Troy or Albany.

ROUTE RETURNING :

Niagara Falls to Ogdensburg.......... { Choice of Routes, via Thousand Islands and Rapids, or all rail.

Ogdensburg to Rouse's Point............Central V't R.R. (O. & L. C. Div.)

Rouse's Point to Burlington............Central Vermont R. R

Burlington to Boston ....Via Excursion No. 123

RATE,   -   -   - $33.40

Excursion No. 125.

BOSTON to NIAGARA FALLS and return.

ROUTE GOING :

Boston to Niagara Falls................ { Choice of Routes via Rutland, Troy or Albany.

ROUTE RETURNING :

Niagara Falls to Montreal.............. { Choice of Routes via Thousand Islands and Rapids, or all rail.

Montreal to St. Johns ....Grand Trunk R'y.

St. Johns to Burlington... ....Central Vermont R. R.

Burlington to Fort Ticonderoga ....Lake Champlain Steamers.

Fort Ticonderoga to Albany, via Saratoga.Del. & Hudson Canal Co's R. R.

Albany to New York....................Hudson River Steamers.

New York to Boston ....Sound Line Steamers

RATE,   -   -   - $35.75

Excursion No. 126.

BOSTON to NIAGARA FALLS and return.

ROUTE GOING :

Boston to Niagara Falls................ { Choice of Routes via Rutland, Troy or Albany.

ROUTE RETURNING :

Niagara Falls to Montreal.............. { Choice of Routes via Thousand Islands and Rapids, or all rail.

Montreal to St. Johns ....Grand Trunk R'y.

St. Johns to Burlington..................Central Vermont R. R.

Burlington to Fort Ticonderoga ....Lake Champlain Steamers.

Fort Ticonderoga to Baldwin.............Del. & Hudson Canal Co's R. R.

Baldwin to Caldwell................. ...Lake George Steamers.

Caldwell to Albany, via Saratoga.........Del. & Hudson Canal Co's R. R.

Albany to New York ....Hudson River Steamers.

New York to Boston ....Sound Line Steamers.

RATE,   · $37.75

111

Excursion No. 127.

BOSTON to NIAGARA FALLS and return.

ROUTE GOING :

Boston to Niagara Falls .... { Choice of Routes via Rutland, Troy or Albany.

ROUTE RETURNING :

Niagara Falls to Montreal............. { Choice of Routes via Thousand Islands and Rapids, or all rail.

Montreal to St. Johns....................Grand Trunk R'y.

St. Johns to Montpelier..................Central Vermont R. R.

Montpelier to Wells River................Montpelier & Wells River R. R.

Wells River to Fabyan's..............Boston & Lowell R. R.(W. M. Div)

Fabyan's to Boston.................... { Choice of Routes via Concord, North Conway or Portland.

RATE,   . $32 65

Excursion No. 128.

BOSTON to NIAGARA FALLS and return.

ROUTE GOING :

Boston to Niagara Falls................ { Choice of Routes via Rutland, Troy or Albany.

ROUTE RETURNING :

Niagara Falls to Ogdensburg......... { Choice of Routes via Thousand Islands and Rapids, or all rail.

Ogdensburg to Rouse's Point........... Central V't R.R. (O. & L. C. Div.)

Rouse's Point to Montpelier............ Central Vermont R. R.

Montpelier to Boston .... { Via Wells River, Fabyan's and Concord, North Conway or Portland.

RATE,   - $31.00

Excursion No. 129.

BOSTON to NIAGARA FALLS and return.

ROUTE GOING :

Boston to Niagara Falls................ { Choice of Routes via Rutland, Troy or Albany.

ROUTE RETURNING :

Niagara Falls to Montreal............. { Choice of Routes via Thousand Islands and Rapids, or all rail.

Montreal to St. Johns....................Grand Trunk R'y.

St. Johns to Montpelier via St. Albans, Waterbury (Mt. Mansfield)......... { Central Vermont R. R.

Montpelier to Wells River.. ....Montpelier & Wells River R. R.

Wells River to Fabyan's ....'...........Boston & Lowell R. R (W. M. Div.)

Fabyan's to Glen Station via Notch.......Portland & Ogdensburg R. R.

Glen Station to Glen House ....Stage.

Glen House to Summit Mt. Washington and return .... { Carriages.

Glen House to Gorham.... ....Stage.

Gorham to Portland..... ....Grand Trunk R'y.

Portland to Boston......................Rail or Steamer.

RATE,   -   - $44.15

Excursion No. 130.

BOSTON to NIAGARA FALLS and return.

ROUTE GOING :

Boston to Niagara Falls............... { Choice of Routes via Rutland, Troy or Albany.

ROUTE RETURNING :

Niagara Falls to Schenectady.............N. Y. Cent. & Hudson River R. R.
Schenectady to Caldwell via Saratoga.....Del. & Hudson Canal Co's R. R.
Caldwell to Baldwin....................Lake George Steamers.
Baldwin to Fort Ticonderoga...........:..Del. & Hudson Canal Co's R. R.
Fort Ticonderoga to Burlington..........Lake Champlain Steamers.
Burlington to White River Junction.......Central Vermont R. R.
White River Junction to Concord.........Boston & Maine R. R.
Concord to Nashua.....................Concord R. R.
Nashua to Boston.....................Boston & Maine R. R.

RATE, - - - $29.75

Excursion No. 131.

BOSTON to NIAGARA FALLS and return.

A Reverse of Excursion No. 130.

RATE, - - - $29.75

Excursion No. 132.

BOSTON to NIAGARA FALLS and return.

ROUTE GOING :

Boston to Nashua ....Boston & Maine R. R.
Nashua to Concord....................Concord R. R.
Concord to White River Junction ....Boston & Maine R. R.
White River Junction to Rouse's Point via { Central Vermont R. R.
  Waterbury and St. Albans ....
Rouse's Point to Ogdensburg ....Central V't R.R. (O. & L. C. Div.)
Ogdensburg to Prescott ....Ferry.
Prescott to Toronto via Alexandria Bay { Rich. & Ontario Navigation Co.
  and Thousand Isles ....
Toronto to Lewiston....................Steamer.
Lewiston to Niagara Falls...............N. Y. Cent. & Hudson River R. R.

ROUTE RETURNING :

Niagara Falls to Boston .... { Choice of Routes via Rutland, Troy or Albany.

RATE, - - - $30.00

Excursion No. 133.

BOSTON to NIAGARA FALLS and return.

ROUTE GOING :

Boston to Ogdensburg....................Via White River Junc. or Rutland.
Ogdensburg to Alexandria Bay...........Steamer.
Alexandria Bay to Clayton ....Steamer.
Clayton to Philadelphia, N. Y............Utica & Black River R. R.
Philadelphia, N. Y., to Lewiston..........Watertown & Ogdensburg R. R.
Lewiston to Niagara Falls...............N. Y. Cent. & Hudson River R. R.

ROUTE RETURNING :

Niagara Falls to Boston .... { Choice of Routes via Rutland, Troy or Albany.

RATE,   -   -   - $30.00

Excursion No. 134.

BOSTON to NIAGARA FALLS and return.

ROUTE GOING :

Boston to Montreal.................. ....Via White River Junc. or Rutland.
Montreal to Toronto via Thousand Isles ....Rich. & Ontario Navigation Co.
Toronto to Lewiston ....Steamer.
Lewiston to Niagara Falls ....N. Y. Cent. & Hudson River R.R.

ROUTE RETURNING :

Niagara Falls to Boston............... { Choice of Routes via Rutland, Troy or Albany.

RATE,   -   - $30.00

SIDE EXCURSIONS.

Sold only in connection with Excursions passing through the first named point.

Excursion No. 250.

UTICA to TRENTON FALLS and return.

Utica to Trenton Falls.................Utica & Black River R. R.
Return same Route.

RATE,   -   .   - $1.00

Excursion No. 251.

BURLINGTON to ST. ALBANS and return.

Burlington to St. Albans and return......Central Vermont R. R.

RATE,   .   - $1.50

Excursion No. 252.

BURLINGTON to AUSABLE CHASM and return.

Burlington to Fort Kent.................Lake Champlain Steamers.
Port Kent to Ausable Chasm.............Stage.
Return same Route.

RATE,   -   -   - $1.50

Excursion No. 253.

BURLINGTON to SARANAC LAKE and return.

Burlington to Plattsburg.................Lake Champlain Steamers.
Plattsburg to Saranac Lake..............Chateaugay R. R.
Return same Route.

RATE,   -   -   - $8.00

Excursion No. 254.

BURLINGTON to PAUL SMITHS and return.

Burlington to Plattsburg..............Lake Champlain Steamers.
Plattsburg to Bloomingdale..............Chateaugay R. R.
Bloomingdale to Paul Smith's............Stage.
Return same Route.

RATE,   - $9.50

Excursion No. 255.

BURLINGTON to MONTREAL and return.

Burlington to St. Johns.................Central Vermont R. R.
St. Johns to Montreal....................Grand Trunk R'y.
Return same Route.
RATE,   -   -   - $5.50

Excursion No. 256.

BURLINGTON to MONTREAL and return, via Ogdensburg.

ROUTE GOING :
Burlington to Rouse's Point.............Central Vermont R. R.
Rouse's Point to Ogdensburg..........Ogdensburg & L. Champlain R. R.
Ogdensburg to Prescott ....Ferry.
Prescott to Montreal via Rapids.........Grand Trunk R'y or Steamer.

ROUTE RETURNING :
Montreal to St. Johns....................Grand Trunk R'y.
St. Johns to Burlington ....Central Vermont R. R.
RATE,   -   -   - $11.50

Excursion No. 257.

ST. ALBANS to CHATEAUGAY CHASM and return.

St. Alban's to Rouse's Point ....Central Vermont R. R.
Rouse's Point to Chateaugay.............Ogdensburg & L. Champlain R. R.
Chateaugay to Chasm....................Coach.
Return same Route.
RATE,   -   -   - $4.00

Excursion No. 258.

WATERBURY to STOWE (Mt. Mansfield) and return.

Waterbury to Stowe (Mt. Mansfield) and ret..Stage.
RATE,   -   -   - $1.00

Excursion No. 259.

WING ROAD to JEFFERSON, N. H. and return.

Wing Road to Whitefield ....Boston & Lowell R. R.
Whitefield to Jefferson....................Whitefield & Jefferson R. R.
Return same Route
RATE,   -   -   - $1.75

Excursion No. 260.

BETHLEHEM JUNCTION to PROFILE HOUSE and return.

Bethlehem Junc. to Profile House and ret... Profile & Franconia Notch R. R.

RATE, - - - $3.00

Excursion No. 261.

BETHLEHEM JUNCTION to BETHLEHEM and return.

Bethlehem Junc. to Bethlehem and ret...... Profile & Franconia Notch R: R.

RATE, - - - $1.00

Excursion No. 262.

FABYAN'S to SUMMIT MT. WASHINGTON and return.

Fabyan's to Base Mt. Washington.......... Boston & Lowell R. R.
Base to Summit Mt. Washington........... Mt. Washington R'y.
Return same Route.

RATE, - - - $6.00

Excursion No. 263.

FABYAN'S to GLEN HOUSE and return.

ROUTE GOING :
Fabyan's to Base Mt. Washington........ Boston & Lowell R. R.
Base to Summit Mt. Washington......... Mt. Washington R'y.
Summit to Glen House................. Carriages.

ROUTE RETURNING :
Glen House to Glen Station... ....Stage.
Glen Station to Fabyan's via Notch.......Portland & Ogdensburg R. R.

RATE, - - - $11.25

Excursion No. 264.

FABYAN'S to CRAWFORD HOUSE and return.

Fabyan s to Crawford House and return... Portland & Ogdensburg R. R.

RATE, - - 60 cents.

Excursion No. 265.

GLEN HOUSE to SUMMIT MT. WASHINGTON and return.

Glen House to Summit Mt. Washington } Carriages.
and Return........................ }

RATE, - - - $5.00

Excursion No. 266.

MONTREAL to LACHINE and return.

ROUTE GOING :
 Montreal to Lachine....................Grand Trunk R'y.

ROUTE RETURNING :
 Lachine to Montreal via Lachine Rapids..Steamer.

RATE,   -   -   -   50 cents.

Excursion No. 267.

MONTREAL to QUEBEC and return.

Montreal to Quebec and return ....Rail or Steamer.

RATE, $5.00

Excursion No. 268.

MONTREAL to ST. LEON SPRINGS and return.

Montreal to Louiseville..................North Shore R'y.
Louiseville to St. Leon Springs...........Stage.
Return same Route.

RATE,   - $3.50

Excursion No. 269

MONTREAL to OTTAWA and return.

ROUTE GOING :
 Montreal to Ottawa......................Rail.

ROUTE RETURNING :
 Ottawa to Prescott......................St. Lawrence & Ottawa R'y.
 Prescott to Montreal via Rapids..........Grand Trunk R'y or Steamer.

RATE,   -   - $7.50

Excursion No. 270.

QUEBEC to SAGUENAY RIVER and return.

Quebec to Ha Ha Bay or Chicoutimi ....St. Lawrence Steam Nav. Co.
Return same Route.

RATE,   -   -   - $8.00

Excursion No. 271.

RIVIERE DU LOUP to SAGUENAY RIVER and return

Riviere du Loup to Ha Ha Bay.........St. Lawrence Steam Nav. Co.

Return same Route.

RATE,   -   -   - $5.50

Excursion No. 272.

OGDENSBURG to ALEXANDRIA BAY and return.

Ogdensburg to Alexandria Bay and Re- } Steamer.
turn via Thousand Isles .... }

RATE,   -   -   - $2.00

EXCURSION RATES

MONTREAL AND RETURN,

———— ALSO ————

Montreal, Quebec and Return.

SUBJECT TO CHANGE.

FOR PARTICULARS INQUIRE OF TICKET AGENT AT POINTS NAMED.

FROM	To MONTREAL AND RETURN.	To QUEBEC AND RETURN.
BOSTON	$16 00	$18 00
CONCORD	14 00	18 00
FALL RIVER	18 40	20 40
HAVERHILL	15 40	18 40
LAWRENCE	15 00	18 00
LOWELL	15 00	18 00
MANCHESTER	14 00	18 00
NASHUA	14 50	18 00
NEW BEDFORD	18 70	20 70
NORWICH	17 00	21 00
PROVIDENCE	18 00	20 00
SPRINGFIELD	15 00	19 00
SALEM	16 00	18 00
WILLIMANTIC	17 00	21 00
WOONSOCKET	17 00	21 00
WORCESTER	16 00	20 00

SPECIAL NOTICES.

Tickets between Toronto, Kingston, Prescott, Montreal and Quebec, are good either boat or rail; also on South Shore Express Steamers from Charlotte. Tickets include meals on Steamers from Toronto to Montreal.

Tickets on the Sound Lines Steamers include a berth.

All other tickets via Steamers are for passage only

Passengers holding Tickets reading via Day Line Steamers on the Hudson River from Albany to New York can have them exchanged at N. Y. C. & H. R.R. Ticket Office in Saratoga, or in Depots at Albany or Troy, for Tickets via RAIL.

Tickets on Hudson River are accepted on the Day Line, the People's Line, and the Citizens' Line Steamers.

Tickets reading over the Mount Washington Railway are not available earlier than about the middle of June, or after about the 20th of September. Passengers should note that many of the steamboat lines cease running or make irregular trips after about the first of October, earlier or later, according to the severity or mildness of the season.

Tourists are allowed to stop over, according to the regulations of the various companies. See following page.

Tickets herein described are good for return trip until October 31st, 1889, inclusive, except when otherwise noted.

Children between five and twelve years of age, half fare; over twelve, full fare.

Purchasers of Summer Excursion Tickets secure all the privileges accorded to passengers holding other First-Class Tickets.

Transfers between stations are not included in Excursion Tickets except where specially noted.

Baggage to the extent of one hundred and fifty (150) pounds will be checked free on Full-Fare Summer Excursion Tickets; and seventy-five (75) pounds on Half-Fare (Children's) Excursion Tickets.

The coupons of tickets reading via Grand Trunk Railway between Niagara Falls and Toronto read by Lewiston and Steamer, but can be exchanged (without extra charge), on application to the agents at Niagara Falls, for tickets via rail to Toronto, Grand Trunk Railway (G. W. Division).

Examine carefully the Side Excursions, and you will find them to embrace many points which are taken to the best advantage in connection with other tours.

If the desired trip is not found herein, please call or write to the office, giving the objective points, as new combinations are constantly made.

Tourists will find that a reliable guide with good maps will add very much to the pleasure of one of their trips. The "PATHFINDER RAILWAY GUIDE" is the cheapest and best official guide, and can be had of any newsdealer for 25 cents, or by addressing "PATHFINDER," Boston.

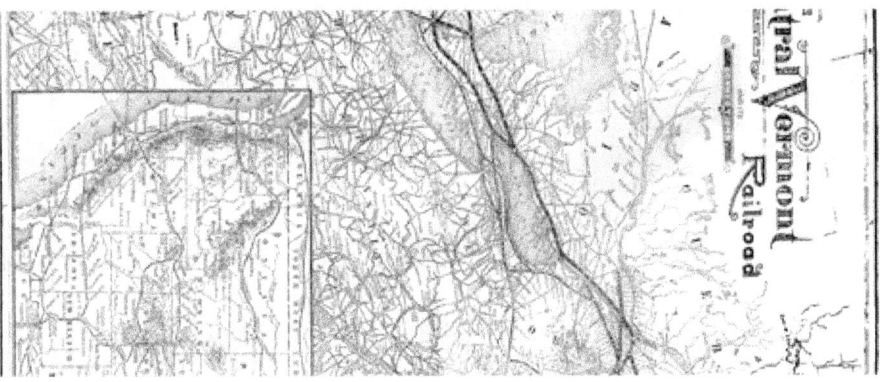

Central Vermont Railroad

TO AGENTS.

NO DEVIATION FROM THE RATES WILL BE ALLOWED WITHOUT SPECIAL AUTHORITY.

Where any Agent who has sold a ticket of this Company's issue, hears from the passenger any just complaint of ill-treatment, the General Officers of this Company would esteem it a favor if the Agent will forward the full particulars of the case, and it shall be promptly investigated.

STOP-OFF PRIVILEGES.

Stop-over privileges extended by the several lines (as noted below) require passengers to take such trains or boats as make stops regularly at the desired stopping-place.

BENNINGTON & RUTLAND R. R.	30 days on notice to conductor.
BOSTON & ALBANY R. R.	No stop-over privileges.
BOSTON, HOOSAC TUNNEL & WEST'N R.R.	On notice to conductor.
BOSTON & LOWELL R. R.	At principal stations.
BOSTON & MAINE R. R.	On notice to conductor.
CANADA ATLANTIC R'Y	On notice to conductor.
CANADIAN PACIFIC R. R.	On notice to conductor.
CENTRAL VERMONT R. R.	On notice to conductor.
CHAMPLAIN TRANSPORTATION LINE (Steamer on Lake Champlain.)	5 days on notice to purser.
CHESHIRE R. R.	30 days on notice to conductor.
CONCORD R. R.	On notice to conductor.
CONNECTICUT RIVER R. R.	On notice to conductor.
DAY LINE STEAMERS (on Hudson River)	10 days on notice to purser.
DELAWARE & HUDSON CANAL CO'S R. R.	On notice to conductor.
EASTERN R. R.	On notice to conductor.
FITCHBURG R. R.	On notice to conductor.
GRAND TRUNK R. R.	On notice to conductor.
INTERCOLONIAL R. R. (or Steamers)	On notice to conductor.
INTERNATIONAL STEAMSHIP LINE	At any landing.
MONTPELIER & WELLS RIVER R. R.	On notice to conductor.
MT. WASHINGTON R. R.	No intermediate stops.
NEW LONDON NORTHERN R. R.	No stop-over privileges.
N. Y. CENTRAL & HUDSON RIVER R. R.	On notice to conductor.
N. Y., NEW HAVEN & HARTFORD R. R.	On notice to conductor.
NORTH SHORE R. R.	No stop-over privileges.
PASSUMPSIC R. R.	On notice to conductor.
PORTLAND & OGDENSBURG R. R.	On notice to conductor.
PROFILE & FRANCONIA NOTCH R. R.	No stop-over privileges.
ROYAL MAIL LINE STEAMERS	On notice to purser.
ST. LAWRENCE & OTTAWA R. R.	No stop-over privileges.
STEAMER ON LAKE GEORGE	5 days on notice to purser.
UTICA & BLACK RIVER R. R.	On notice to conductor.
VERMONT VALLEY R. R.	On notice to conductor.

HOTELS AND SUMMER BOARDING HOUSES.

RUTLAND DIVISION.

LOCATION.	Name of House.	Post-Office.	Proprietor.	Distance from Station.	Capacity.	Price per Day.	Price per Week.	Altitude above sea.	Conveyance.
Bellows Falls, Vt.	Island House	Bellows Falls	C. W. Towns	30 rods	75	$2 50	$14 00	250	
	Town's Hotel	"	C. W. Towns	30 "	100	2 50	10 00	196	
	Commercial House	"	Ladd & Nims	38 "	50	2 00	9 00	259	
	Saxton's River	Saxton's River	M. A. Wilder	5 miles	85	1 50	8 00	410	Stage.
	Phelps House	Grafton	F. & H. Phelps	12 "	80	1 50	8 00	1269	Stage.
Chester, Vt.	Chester House	Chester	J. L. Sanborn	8 rods	40	2 00	10 00	518	
	Lowell Lake House	"	G. H. Hilton	13 miles	75	2 00	10 00	1118	Private.
	Londonderry House	Londonderry	J. P. Farwell	15 "	35	2 00	8 00	1008	Stage.
	Highland House	Weston	D. D. Waite	13 "	40	2 00	8 00	1126	Stage.
Gassett's, Vt.	Eagle House	Perkinsville	G. Alford	3 miles	30	1 25	6 00	633	Stage.
	Springfield House	Springfield	W. Miner	8 "	30	1 25	6 00	633	Stage.
Proctorsville, Vt.	Eagle Hotel	Proctorsville	E. E. Cross	30 rods	35	1 50	4 00	848	
Ludlow, Vt.	Ludlow House	Ludlow	E. P. Warner	½ mile	50	2 00	7 to 9	943	Private.
	Mayo's	"	G. S. Bridge	½ "	55	1 50	4 50 & 50	943	Private.
	Echo Lake Hotel	Tyson	E. P. Warner	5 miles	75	2 00	8 to 10	1236	Stage.
	Wilder's	Plymouth Union	D. P. Wilder	10 "	40	1 00	4 to 5	1306	Stage.
Mt. Holly, Vt.	Mechanicsville	Mechanicsville	E. R. Chase	2 miles	12	1 50	3 00	1798	
East Wallingford, Vt.	E. W. Hotel	East Wallingford	J. Todd	15 rods	25	2 00	4 00	1062	
Cuttingsville, Vt.	Union House	Cuttingsville	D. K. Butterfield	90 rods	50	1 50	3 00		Private.
	Farm House	"	H. F. Partridge	3½ miles	15		3 00		Private.

LOCATION	Name of House	Post-Office	Proprietor	Distance from Station	Capacity	Price per Day	Price per Week	Altitude above sea	Conveyance
Rutland, Vt.	Bates House	Rutland	A. H. Tuttle & Son	10 rods	150	$1 50	$12 00	324	
	Bardwell House	"	Crompton & Carpenter	10 "	125	2 50	12 00	324	
	Berwick	"	W. H. Valiquette	15 "	125	2 00	10 00	324	
	Killington Peak	"	C. Maynshoffer	10 miles	40	2 50	12 00	2000	Stage.
	Numerous private boarding places								
Poultney, Vt.	Montvert House	Middletown Springs	J. Kuper	3 miles	150	2 50	10 to 15		Private.
	Lake View House	Poultney	P. Griffith	2 "	100	2 00	10 00		
West Rutland, Vt.	Barnes House	West Rutland	F. Gorham	6 rods	75	2 00	10 00	500	
	Clarendon Springs House	Clarendon Springs	Murray Bros.	4 miles	75	2 50	10 00	500	Stage.
Pittsford, Vt.	Otter Creek Hotel	Pittsford	J. Forvas	½ mile	50	2 00	7 to 10	474	Private.
Brandon, Vt.	Hyde Hotel	Sudbury	A. W. Hyde	3 miles	200	2 00	8 to 14	623	Stage.
	Brandon House	Brandon	Cox & Mack	60 rods	75	2 00	7 to 10	364	Stage.
	Lake Dunmore House	Salisbury	F. Kupper	8 miles	100	2 50	8 to 15	364	Stage.
Ticonderoga, N. Y.	Rogers Rock Hotel	Rogers Rock	Treadway Bros.	6 miles	150	3 00	14 to 21	146	Private.
	Burleigh House	Ticonderoga	D. J. Gilligan	2 "	200	2 00	8 to 14	150	
	Halls House	"	Mrs. C. A. Caswell	1½	150	2 00	6 to 12	150	Private.
Larabee's Point, Vt.	Lake House	Larabee's Point	Mrs. A. C. Fay	½ mile	75	2 00	8 to 12	96	
Salisbury, Vt.	Lake Dunmore House	Salisbury	F. Kupper	5 miles	100		8 to 15	959	Stage.
Middlebury, Vt.	Pierce House	Middlebury	F. W. Pierce	½ mile	50	1 75	6 to 9	324	
	Addison House	"	J. Higgins	1½ "	50	2 00	7 to 10	324	
	Beadleaf Inn	Beadleaf	J. Duttit	12 miles	100	3 00	10 to 14	1600	Stage.
New Haven, Vt.	Parish Hotel	New Haven	W. M. Parish	1½ miles	50	2 00	8 00	284	Stage.
	Bristol House	Bristol	J. J. Ridley	3½ "	50	2 00	8 00	284	Stage.
	Commercial Hotel	"	R. F. Hatch	3½ "	25	2 00	8 00	284	
Vergennes, Vt.	Stevens House	Vergennes	S. S. Gaines	½ mile	150	2 50	7 to 10	194	Private.
	American House	"	C. H. Colston	½ "	50	2 50	6 00	150	Private.
North Ferrisburg, Vt.	Martin House	North Ferrisburg	S. B. Martin	1½ miles	50	2 00	3 00	124	Private.

Place	House	Post Office	Proprietor	Distance				
North Ferrisburg, Vt.	Brookside Inn	North Ferrisburg	M. L. Richardson	2½ miles	10	$3 00	$5 00		Private.
Burlington, Vt.	Van Ness	Burlington	Drew & Clark, Manag'r	¼ mile	175	2 to 3 50	....	200	
	Rowe	"	R. McNulty		20	2 00	....	100	
	Burlington House	"	Delaney & Harrington		100	2 & 2 5	....	4 0	
	Numerous private boarding places.								
Winooski, Vt.	Stevens	Winooski	James Evarts	½ mile	30	1 00	7 00	165	

CENTRAL DIVISION.

Place	House	Post Office	Proprietor	Distance				
White River Junction, Vt.	Junction House	W. R. Junction	Lavender & Eddy	20 rods	150	$2 00	$10 00	364	Private.
Hartford, Vt.	White River	Hartford	C. W. Pease	¼ mile	75	2 00	7 00	400	Stage.
Sharon, Vt.	Manley's	Sharon	F. M. Manley	½ mile	40	1 00	3 00	507	Private
South Royalton, Vt.	South Royalton House	South Royalton	C. B. Woodard		50	2 00	7 00	504	Private.
	Orange Co.	Chelsea	E. D. Barnes	14 miles	75	2 00	5 00	900	Stage.
Royalton, Vt.	Cascadnac House	Royalton	O. C. Severns	30 rods	30	1 50	2 to 3	512	Private.
Bethel, Vt.	Wilson House	Bethel	J. D. Lawrence	20 rods	10	1 50	2 to 12	931	Private.
	Bascom House	"	R. Gibson	20 "	20	1 00	5 00	532	Private.
	Locust Creek House	"	G. T. McLaughlin	4 miles	15	1 50	2 to 9	600	Stage.
	Silver Lake House	Barnard	C. E. French	8 "	30	....	7 to 10 50	4372	Private.
	Rochester House	Rochester	O. M. Ford	18 "	25	2 00	6 to 8	1471	Private.
	Hancock House	Hancock	J. E. Wright	22 "	25	2 00	6 to 8	1273	Private.
Randolph, Vt.	Red Lion Inn	West Randolph	Mrs. E. A. Phillips	6 rods	30	2 00	7 to 10	638	Private.
	Valley Farm	"	A. B. Manchester	1 mile	20	2 00	7 to 10	598	Private.
	Griswold	"	F. Griswold	30 rods	10	....	3 to 12	698	Private.
	Parish	Randolph Centre	L. Parish	4 miles	20	....	7 to 10	1300	Private.
	Randolph House	"	L. Murphy	3½ "	30	....	3 to 7	1900	Stage.
Braintree, Vt.	Private	West Braintree	L. Fish	40 rods	13	2 00	4 00	779	
	Private	Hancock	Mrs. F. Wright	10 miles	2	2 00	6 00	1100	
	Private	Granville	L. L. Udell	3 "	10	2 00	6 00	900	
Roxbury, Vt.	Nannck	Roxbury	M. E. Farrington	10 rods	20	2 00	5 00	1000	

LOCATION.	Name of House.	Post-Office.	Proprietor.	Distance from Station.	Capacity.	Price per Day.	Price per Week.	Attendance (per cent)	Conveyance
Montpelier, Vt.	Pavilion	Montpelier	J. S. Vilas	5 rods	150	$3 50	$10 to 15	300	Stage.
	Montpelier House	"	Geo. Wheeler	60 "	125	1 50	7 00	300	
	Union House	"	A. A. Kelton	75 "	200	1 50	10 00	300	
	Riverside	"	H. Fullerton	50 "	25	1 00	5 to 7	300	
	Lake View House	South Woodbury	A. H. Holt	13 miles	25	1 00	5 to 7	150	
	Numerous private boarding places.								
Barre, Vt.	Central	Barre	F. Haydon	½ mile	50	1 50	8 00	50	
	Hotel Barre	"	H. A. Rugg		200	2 00	7 to 14	150	
Middlesex, Vt.	Washington	Middlesex	A. R. Kisher	60 rods	15	1 50	7 00	150	
	Waitsfield House	Waitsfield	A. W. Bigelow	11 miles	15	1 50	7 00	90	
Waterbury, Vt.	Waterbury House	Waterbury	B. Barrett & Son	15 rods	100	2 50	7 to 12	100	
	Mt. Mansfield	Stowe	S. Gurney	10 miles	400	2 50	10 to 14	500	
	Village Hotel	Waterbury	F. D. Griffith	60 rods	40	1 50	7 00	150	
Bolton, Vt.	Bishop House	Bolton	M. H. Bishop	10 rods	25	2 00	7 00	150	
Jonesville, Vt.	Jonesville House	Jonesville	F. B. Gillett	10 rods	25		5 00	50	
	Private	"	Mrs. Douglass	25 "	10		4 to 5	25	
Richmond, Vt.	Bellevue House	Richmond	G. W. Maydig	30 rods	15	2 00	4 00	150	Private.
Essex Junction, Vt.	Central House	Essex Junction	F. F. Shepard	3 rods	25	2 00	7 00	150	Private.
	Junction House	"	Z. Haggood	25 "	25	1 50	8 00	150	Private.
Colchester, Vt.	Mallett's Bay House	Mallett's Bay	F. Coley	3 miles	75	1 00	6 to 12	90	Private.
Milton, Vt.	Elm Tree House	Milton	P. Mansfield	90 rods	25	1 00	4 to 8	100	Private.
	Hotel Proctor	"	Wm. Lunden	5 "	25	1 00	5 to 10	150	Private.
Georgia, Vt.	Valley Hotel	Fairfax	J. Shedd	4 miles	10	1 00	4 to 6	100	Stage.
	Allred House	"	D. C. Currie		10	1 00	4 to 6	100	Stage.
	Franklin House	Georgia Centre	O. Kimpton	¼ "	10	1 00	4 to 6	400	Private.
St. Albans, Vt.	Weldon House	St. Albans	F. A. Beebe	40 rods	250	2 00	10 to 15	400	
	American House	"	S. L S road	25 "	100	2 50	7 to 14	400	
	Numerous private boarding places.								

WESTERN DIVISION.

Swanton, Vt	Central House	Swanton	J. F. Kelly	¾ mile	30	$4.50	$5.00	144	Private.
	Champlain House	"	D. J. Merrill	2 miles	175	2.50	17.00	120	
	American House	"	A. P. Herrick	20 rods	40	2.50	5.00	140	
Alburgh Springs, Vt	Missisco House	Alburgh Springs	C. Smith	1½ miles	100		5 to 15	130	Private.
	Alburgh Springs House	"	L. E. Brooks	1½ "	200		5 to 25	150	Private.
Rouse's Point, Vt	Holland House	Rouse's Point	A. E. Barrett	½ mile	30	2.00	5.00	100	Private.
	Massachusetts	"	J. Cogan	½ "	30	2.00	5.00	100	Private.
	Windsor	"	Chas. F. Beck	½ "	100	2.00	14.00	100	Private.
	Frontier	"	Mrs. C. Lewis	20 rods	40	2.00	5.00	100	Private.

NORTHERN DIVISION.

Highgate Springs, Vt	Franklin House	Highgate Springs	J. L. Scott		125	$4.50	$10 to $20	125	Private.
	Elmwood Cottage	"	R. Phelps	90 rods	30	2.50	7 to 10	30	
	Lake House	"	J. L. Scott	100 "	50	2.50	10 to 12		
St. Armand, P. Q	Shelters	Saint Armand	A. Shelters		25	1.00	3 to 4	175	Private.
	Canada Hotel	"	N. L. Paquet		25	1.00	3 to 4	175	
	Lake View	Phillipsburg	E. W. McKanney	2 miles	30	1.00	3 to 4	120	Stage.
	Champlain House	"	E. C. Bark	2 "	100	2.50	5 to 7		Private.

MISSISQUOI VALLEY DIVISION.

Sheldon Springs, Vt	Congress Hall	Sheldon Springs	Miss E. Finch	25 rods	125	$1.50	$10 to $15	900	Private.
Sheldon, Vt	Portland	Sheldon	A. C. Marvin	2 miles	30	1.50	4.00	150	Private.

LOCATION.	Name of House.	Post Office.	Proprietor.	Distance from Station.	Capacity.	Price per Day.	Price per Week.	Altitude above sea.	Conveyance
Champlain, N. Y.	Champlain House	Champlain, N. Y.	J. L. Matteson	80 rods	40	$2 00	$8 00	100	
	Private	" "	S. M. Burroughs	40 "	5	...	10 00	130	
	Mansion House	" "	V. Plummer	30 "	5	...	10 00	130	
Mooers Junction, N. Y.	Commercial House	Mooers Jc., N. Y.	W. S. Farmer	40 "	15	1 00	6 to 8	250	
Mooers Forks, N. Y.	Rivers Side	Mooers' Forks.	Wm. L. Armstrong	60 "	100	1 00	5 00	350	
	Irwin	"	G. H. Sennans	100 "	50	1 50	5 00	300	
	Crawford	"	T. Crawford	15 "	100	1 00	8 00	350	
Ellenburgh, N. Y.	Boynton	Ellenburgh Depot	Boynton & Smith	3 "	12–15	1 00	3 50 to 5	750	
	American	"	P. Lafayette	25 "	12–15	...	3 50 to 5	750	
	Ellenburgh	Ellenburgh.	Danisny & Thayer	1½ miles	15–20	...	3 50 to 5	750	
	Clinton	Ellenburgh Centre	H. Baker	5 "	10–15	...	3 50 to 5	1050	
Churubusco, N. Y.	Churubusco House	Churubusco	J. W. Anderson	40 rods	15	1 00	5 00	1040	
Chateaugay, N. Y.	Chasm	Chateaugay, Clinton Co.	Chat. Chasm Co.	1½ miles	75–100	2 25	10 to 14	975	
	Ralphs	Lyon Mountain	J. W. Hutton	15 "	75–100	2 50	10 to 16	1700	
	Merrill's	Merrill	Merrill Bros.	15 "	50	2 50 to 2	3 00 to	1300	
	Bellows	Chateaugay Lake	M. S. Bellows	8 "	25	2 00	7 00	1300	
	Indian Point	Merrill	R. M. Shutts	15 "	30	1 50	8 to 10	1300	
	Riverside Cottage	Chateaugay Lake	H. S. Farnsworth	6 "	20	1 25	6 to 10	1300	
Malone, N. Y.	Ayers House	Duane	W. L. Ayers	15 "	75	2 00	8–10	1700	
	Mountain View House	Malone	R. G. Lowe	12 "	40	2 00	10 00	1500	
	Lake Meacham House	Malone or Duane	A. R. Fuller	26 "	400–50	2 00	10 to 15	1500	
	Loon Lake House	Loon Lake	Ferd. W. Chase	20 "	375	3 00	10 50 to 17 50	1800	
	Paul Smith's	Paul Smith's	A. A. Smith	20 "	300	3 00	17 50	1700	
Brushton, N. Y.	Brushton	Brushton	Wood Bros	20 rods	30	1 00	4 to 5	460	
Lawrence, N. Y.	Union House	North Lawrence.	Jas. Caul	10 rods	50	1 00	3 00	600	
	Commercial House.	"	F. P. Norris	15 "	75	1 00	5 00	600	
	Central	Lawrenceville	M. V. Barney	3 miles	50	1 00	3 00	600	

Lawrence, N. Y.	Commercial	Nicholville	T. B. Smith & Son	1 mile	50	$1.25	$4.00	600
	Cook	Hopkinton	C. Murphy	5 "	25	1.00	3.00	600
	Blow	Fort Jackson	M. P. Blow	5 "	25	1.00	3.00	600
Norwood, N. Y.	Whitney	Norwood, N. Y.	S. R. Phelps	100 rods		2.00	11.00	300
	American	"	J. R. Perr	2 "		2.00	10.00	300
Saranac Springs	Hatfield House	Hatfield, N. Y.	Hatfield Bros.	½ mile	100	2.50	10 to 14	300
	White's Hotel	Malone, N. Y.	S. S. Danforth	33 "	2.00	8.50 to 11	300
	Allen House	"	D. W. Beardsley	4 "	40	2.50	8.00	300
	Bentley House	Hatfield, N. Y.	M. Hauck	½ "	50	2.00	9.00	300
	Harrington House	"	W. R. Stearns	40 "	1.50	7.00 to 10	300
	E. M. Smith	"	E. M. Smith	½ "	25	1.50	7.00 to 10	300
	Woodke House	"		½ "	25	1.50	7.00	300
	Numerous private boarding houses							
Dickinson Centre	Cross House	"	M. A. Davis	60 rods	25	1.25	5.00	200
St. Regis Falls, N. Y.	Waverly House	St. Regis Falls	L. C. Goodrich	At Station	50	2.00	8.00	1500
	Mountain View House	Everton, N. Y.	D. J. McNeal, Jr.	9 miles	35	1.50	6.00	1800
	Trout Lake House	St. Regis Falls	A. Prentice	10 "	25	1.00	5.00	1500
Spring Cove	Blue Mountain House	"	H. Phelps	5 "	40	1.50	8.00	2100
Paul Smith's, N. Y.	Paul Smith's	Paul Smith's	A. A. Smith	5 "	300	3.00	7.50	7300

BRATTLEBORO AND WHITEHALL DIVISIONS.

West Dummerston	Valley House	West Dummerston	H. H. Norcross	50 rods	20	$1.00	$4.50	
Newfane, N. Y.	Fayetteville House	Newfane	S. Worcester	30 "	10	1.00	5.00	
	County House	"	Geo. Underwood	15 "	15	1.00	5.00	
Jamaica	Jamaica House	Jamaica	L. J. Strong	½ mile	30	2.00	6.00	30
Londonderry	Brandy	Peru, Vt.	G. K. Davis	6 "	50	2.00	8.00	600
	Nixon	Londonderry	D. D. Walt & Son	4 "	60		5.00 to 9	300
	Londonderry	"	J. P. Farwell	5 "	60		5.00	800
	Morgan	Brandville	Mrs. J. Morgan	5 "	50	1.50	6.00	400
	Edgewater Park	South Londonderry	Tara Farnery	20 rods	50	2.00	8.00	Level
	Lowell Lake	Chester, Vt.	G. H. Filtow	4 miles	50	2.00	7.00	200
	Huntley	North Windham	Chester Huntley	4 "	20		4.00	500

———AND———

Information Relative Thereto Apply to

T. H. HANLEY, - - - - - Ticket Agent,
260 Washington Street, Boston.

W. RAYMOND, - - - - Gen'l Excursion Agent,
296 Washington Street, Boston.

E. R. COPPINS, - - - - Passenger Agent,
317 Broadway, New York.

A. C. STONEGRAVE, - Canadian Passenger Agent,
136 St. James Street, Montreal.

———

CHARLES LALIME, - - - - - N. E. Agent,
Worcester, Mass.

F. B. CILLEY, - - - - - - Advertising Agent,
260 Washington Street, Boston.

E. H. HUGHES, - - - - - Western Passenger Agent,
C. & G. T. R'y Office, 103 So. Clark St., Chicago, Ill.

Also at the principal Ticket Offices of the Pennsylvania R. R.; Philadelphia & Reading R. R.; Baltimore & Ohio R. R.; New York Central & Hudson River R. R.; New York, New Haven & Hartford R. R.; New York, Lake Erie & Western R. R.; New York, West Shore & Buffalo R'y; Fall River, Providence, Stonington and Norwich Lines; Thomas Cook & Son (Head Office, 261 Broadway, N. Y.); Grand Trunk R'y; Rome, Watertown & Ogdensburg R. R.; Utica & Black River R. R., and at the offices of the principal New England Roads.

———

J. W. HOBART,
General Manager,

S. W. CUMMINGS,
Gen'l Passenger Agent,

GENERAL OFFICES, ST. ALBANS, VT.